Letters of the great artists

from Blake to Pollock

LETTERS
of the great artists

from Blake to Pollock

RICHARD FRIEDENTHAL

152 plates, 59 in colour

RANDOM HOUSE · NEW YORK

The letters were translated by Daphne Woodward
with the exceptions detailed in the
Sources and References

CONTENTS

This second volume of our anthology of artists' letters covers the period from the early nineteenth century to the present day. In contrast to earlier centuries, when only a few artists expressed themselves fluently in writing, the material now becomes more abundant. Even in modern times, however, there are many examples of those who prefer to work quietly in their studios like the painters of an older epoch, having neither taste nor talent for putting their ideas into writing, much less for laying down a programme. This does not necessarily mean that such men are cut off from the trends of contemporary thought; for an important part is played by the discussion of work in progress and by the talk that goes on in cafés – those most important institutions, particularly in the artistic life of Paris.

But there are also painters with a decided gift for expressing themselves on paper, just as, among musicians, Berlioz, Schumann, Wagner and Liszt were eloquent in setting forth their views on their art in literary essays, articles and private letters. Artists of this sort first emerged among the Romantics, who were the earliest to group themselves deliberately into a 'movement' instead of a 'school' centred on some great painter's studio, as in previous centuries. Since then, the world of art has experienced a succession of movements and counter-movements – which in recent years have followed one another with such rapidity as to require a running commentary of explanation and interpretation. The artist is no longer the sole interpreter of his own work. The art critic, who was formerly a writer in some field of literature other than criticism, like the poet Baudelaire, has now become an influential authority even exerting a certain influence upon the artists themselves. It is interesting to note how in the early days of Impressionism, for example, it was this critical circle that produced vigorous pronouncements on

7

theory, while at first the painters themselves 'merely' looked at the world in their own novel way and put down what they saw on canvas. At the same time, however, closer contact began to be established between the painters and the other representatives of the creative arts – chiefly in the great meltingpot of Paris, but elsewhere as well. Painting was even influenced by science, as evidenced by the Pointillistes, whose methods were inspired by certain discoveries resulting from scientific research. Thus, trends in modern art are prompted not only by the personal friendships formed by painters and sculptors with poets, composers and authors, but also by certain aims that they all have in common. The written programme, manifesto or pronunciamento and the detailed exposition of theories are becoming more and more important. But interesting as many of these documents are, space forbids their inclusion in this anthology, especially as in most cases they are of considerable length; for to cut them down to a brief outline frequently gives a distorted view of their author's intentions, as has often been seen in the past.

In these pages the chief stress has been laid on the artists' personal utterances, in an attempt to bring out the highly important influence of the experiences they went through in life. Early in the nineteenth century the artist became his own master, which had previously been the case only with the rare, outstanding genius. He continued for a long time to be dependent on commissions and thus compelled, to some extent, to fall in with the views of his patron – particularly when dealing with that most difficult of all patrons, the State or some public authority. But he made increasing demands for complete independence; and his right to it was eventually recognized. Artists in general began to enjoy an established and often brilliant social position. The 'princely painter', with his fine house and great fortune, was no longer an exception, like Titian; he and his kind could be counted in dozens – though many of their names have now receded into the background of art history. At the same time, as an inevitable feature of this new independence, there were the solitaries, disdained except by a narrow circle of friends. William Blake is perhaps the earliest of these lonely visionaries; it was half a century or more before he began to be appreciated. There were those, including most of the Impressionists, who had a hard struggle at the beginning. There were those who met an early death, sometimes at their own hand like Van Gogh, and those who took to flight, like Gauguin. And though most of them led retired lives, contemporary history broke in upon them at times, since it is not only in art that revolutions occur. In 1871 Courbet was swept into the 'Commune', and in the

First World War an entire generation of promising young artists was wiped out, leaving no written evidence of their existence except for a few letters by Franz Marc and others.

Incidentally, a warning may not be out of place here: the artist is not always the best commentator on his own work or the best expounder of his own views. He may be mistaken. Sometimes the work is greater than its creator can say or than his contemporaries perceive. But we thought it better to let these writings speak for themselves rather than overload them with commentaries. Their purpose is to lead the reader to the artists and their work. And we hope that this selection will help to give a clearer view of one of the most varied and fruitful periods in the development of art.

R.F.

'. . . I do not consider myself at work
unless I am before a six-foot canvas',
*wrote John Constable to a friend. This sketch
is from one of his letters.*

THE EARLY NINETEENTH
CENTURY

WILLIAM BLAKE TO WILLIAM HAYLEY

London, 7 October 1803

Dear Sir,
Your generous & tender solicitude about your devoted rebel makes it
absolutely necessary that he should trouble you with an account of his
safe arrival, which will excuse his begging the favor of a few lines to
inform him how you escaped the contagion of the Court of Justice – I
fear that you have & must suffer more on my account than I shall ever
be worth – Arrived safe in London, my wife in very poor health, still I
resolve not to lose hope of seeing better days.

Art in London flourishes. Engravers in particular are wanted. Every
Engraver turns away work that he cannot execute from his super-
abundant Employment. Yet no one brings work to me. I am content
that it shall be so as long as God pleases. I know that many works of a
lucrative nature are in want of hands; other Engravers are courted. I
suppose that I must go a Courting, which I shall do awkwardly; in
the meantime I lose no moment to complete Romney to satisfaction.

How is it possible that a Man almost 50 years of Age, who has not
lost any of his life since he was five years old without incessant labour &
study, how is it possible that such a one with ordinary common sense can
be inferior to a boy of twenty, who scarcely has taken or deigns to take
pencil in hand, but who rides about the Parks or saunters about the
Playhouses, who Eats & drinks for business not for need, how is it

13

possible that such a fop can be superior to the studious lover of Art can scarcely be imagin'd. Yet such is somewhat like my fate & such it is likely to remain. Yet I laugh & sing, for if on Earth neglected I am in heaven a Prince among Princes, & even on Earth beloved by the Good as a Good Man; this I should be perfectly contented with, but at certain periods a blaze of reputation arises round me in which I am consider'd as one distinguished by some mental perfection, but the flame soon dies again & I am left stupified and astonish'd. O that I could live as others do in a regular succession of Employment, this wish I fear is not to be accomplish'd to me – Forgive this Dirge-like lamentation over a dead horse, & now I have lamented over the dead horse let me laugh & be merry with my friends till Christmas, for as Man liveth not by bread alone, I shall live altho I should want bread – nothing is necessary to me but to do my Duty & to rejoice in the exceeding joy that is always poured out on my Spirit, to pray that my friends & you above the rest may be made partakers of the joy that the world cannot conceive, that you may still be replenish'd with the same & be as you always have been, a glorious & triumphant Dweller in immortality. Please to pay for me my best thanks to Miss Poole: tell her that I wish her a contented Excess of Happiness – some say that Happiness is not Good for Mortals, & they ought to be answer'd that Sorrow is not fit for Immortals & is utterly useless to any one; a blight never does good to a tree, & if a blight kill not a tree but it still bear fruit, let none say that the fruit was in consequence of the blight. When this Soldier-like danger is over I will do double the work I do now, for it will hang heavy on my Devil who terribly resents it; but I soothe him to peace, & indeed he is a good natur'd Devil after all & certainly does not lead me into scrapes – he is not in the least to be blamed for the present scrape, as he was out of the way all the time on other employment seeking amusement in making Verses, to which he constantly leads me very much to my hurt & some-times to the annoyance of my friends; as I percieve he is now doing the same work by my letter, I will finish it, wishing you health & joy in God our Saviour.

To Eternity yours,
Wllm Blake

William Blake (1757–1827) worked in almost complete isolation, cut off not only from society but even from his fellow artists, known and appreciated by a mere handful of friends and not 'discovered' until half a century after his death. His friendship with Hayley dated from 1800 when they were neighbours in Sussex. Hayley was writing his 'Life of Cowper' and Blake engraved the illustrations. The reference to 'Romney' is to the engraving of the head of the artist that Blake was doing for Hayley's 'Life', but which was not used.

At the time of this letter Blake had already begun making experiments with copperplate engraving in connection with his own creative work. These took the form of poems surrounded by imaginative illustrations coloured by hand. 'Songs of Innocence' was published in this way in 1789. In a letter written towards the end of his life he gives a price-list:

WILLIAM BLAKE TO DAWSON TURNER

London, 9 June 1818

			£	s.	d.
. . . Songs of Innocence	28 Prints	Octavo	3	3	0
Songs of Experience	26 do.	Octavo	3	3	0
Urizen	28 Prints	Quarto	5	5	0
Milton	50 do.	Quarto	10	10	0

. . . The few I have printed & Sold are sufficient to have gained me great reputation as an Artist, which was the chief thing Intended. But I have never been able to produce a Sufficient number for a general Sale by means of a regular Publisher. It is therefore necessary to me that any Person wishing to have any or all of them should send me their Order to Print them on the above terms, & I will take care that they shall be done at least as well as any I have yet Produced.

HENRY FUSELI TO JOHANN KASPAR LAVATER

Rome, March 1775

Thank you for the books, and here is a little gossip. As I suspected, I had read some Klopstock already, and in a less affected style, which is what pleases me about his Odes, and what must please people of discernment in all periods, and all sensitive souls. May God take the greater number of his lofty, devotional odes, brought together again out of Kramer's weekly journal, and the Devil take nearly all his Teutonic mythology! It is a lie to say that the greater part of the Psalms of David are poetic – and that for the very same reason on which Klopstock bases the alleged superiority of his own and other German poetry to the English; viz., that most of the Psalms arise out of a personal sentiment, a particular place, or some other emotional fancy. Will anyone tell me that stale stuff like the 119th Psalm, or one of Klopstock's pieces with their perpetual cries of 'Lord, Lord', is poetry? Pictures – the pictures that you (not you personally – the Germans, and the Swiss as well) despise, the pictures you cannot invent – are painted by Homer, the father of all poetry. Homer, and Deborah's song and the Book of Job – those are the kind of things that establish the value of feelings. A sincere, general, lively feeling flows through such pictures into all hearts, whereas the spurious, parochial, individual ones can appeal only to a few, and in certain times and places, while causing perplexity and bewilderment to all others. What an indescribable difference there is between the truth and strength of feeling that penetrates into all hearts from Sappho's *Phainetai*, from some of Haller's love-songs, or even from these little-known lines:

> *So oft des Nachts mein' Ader schlägt,*
> *Soll dich mein Geist umfangen*

and the tame confusion and apoplectic affectation with which an artificial longing for Cidli is worked up for your benefit? The *facultas lacrimatoria*, that beauty-spot on the face of German poetry from Klopstock's heights to the depths of Dusch, the telescoped eyes, the ineffable glances and the entire theological hermaphroditism, are more perishable rags than the ones they are printed upon. Feel that kind of thing, if you like; I used to imagine I felt it myself, as a child; but it is sheer impudence to parade it in front of other people, and if it is in your pious poems, then I say, like Götz von Berlichingen: For the majesty of religion I have all due reverence, but you, Sir Captain, whatever your name may be, you can kiss my arse – and I shut the window with a bang!

At this very moment I have received your whining, faint-hearted letter!

So far as concerns Klopstock's patriotic poetry, with the exception of 'Hermann und Thusnelde' and the two 'Muses', I say again, 'the Devil take it! . . .' The contempt I feel for Klopstock's taste in painting, when he talks about Preissler or the Germans, resembles the arrogance with which he judges the English. His ignorance of their poetry is ludicrous. Citizens – Fatherland – Freedom – if at least he were Swiss – but where is the fatherland of a German? – Is it in Swabia, Brandenburg, Austria or Saxony? Is it in the marshes that swallowed up the Roman Legions and Varus? Did Rome ever lose a battle fought on decent, solid ground? A Frenchman (curse him!) has more right to talk about his 'fatherland' than a fellow from Quedlinburg or Osnabrück or any other puffed-up toad-spawn crawling between Rügen and Ulm. What has a lackey to be proud of? Of his master's livery? And which one? The first, second or third? Freedom, God! Freedom from Christian's flatterer!

The English do not credit themselves with having produced a single poet in this century, unless it be Richardson. Thomson's catalogue, so often translated among you, Young's pyramids of dough, Pope's rhymed and scanning prose, they do not regard as poetry, any more than they would vouchsafe that name to Wieland's or Gessner's lachrymose sweetmeats – so God help you!

Drawings, and such as I promised you, you shall have; it was not possible within the appointed time, because I was then obliged to finish a painting. But so as not to keep you waiting too long, I will send them to you in threes or fours. You can imagine what a delightful pastime it is for me to have to make copies of my own ideas. No one else can do it for me.

P.S. You may leave out *très-célèbre* before the word *peintre*, that sort of thing is just German foolishness.

Fuseli was born a Swiss (Heinrich Füssli) in 1741. He studied art in Germany, then came to England in 1763 and worked as translator and illustrator. In 1770 he went to Rome and stayed for eight years, copying the Michelangelo frescoes of the Sistine Chapel. When he came back to England he began painting in a nightmarish style that eventually brought him fame. He became a Royal Academician in 1790 and Keeper of the Royal Academy in 1804. Wilkie, Etty, Haydon and Landseer were among his many pupils. A revolutionary spirit all his life, he was a merciless critic of art and politics, with a mordant prose style of his own. The foregoing letter is written in the manner of the German 'Sturm und Drang' movement, to which he had leanings at the time. Goethe and Herder copied this letter as a kind of manifesto and showed it to their friends. Essentially, however, Fuseli belongs to no movement at all; he may be called a Romantic, some decades before the Romantic movement existed; and in recent times he has been claimed as an ancestor by the Surrealists.

Johann Kaspar Lavater, to whom this letter is addressed, was a Zürich pastor, now chiefly remembered for his famous 'Physiognomische Fragmente'. Fuseli's criticism of Klopstock, then at the height of his fame as a poet and the idol of German youth, is characteristic of his independent mind.

HENRY FUSELI TO MADAME ORELL IN ZÜRICH

Namur, 18 April 1779

I sent you a hurried note from Mulhouse; unless the innkeeper was a scoundrel, you must have received it by now. I regret to say that all my friends appear to be more neglectful about writing than I am – although this reveals to me another virtue in myself; with God's help I may yet become quite perfect.

Here I sit, dear Orell, in a town full of soldiers, parsons, coal-crushers, landladies and shop-girls, with my head propped on both fists and my eyes now filled with tears and now rolling, and listen to a raven under my window that squawks 'Cuckoo' and 'Who's there?' Who is there?

'. . . the pictures you cannot invent – are painted by Homer, the father of all poetry.' *Fuseli's painting of 'Thetis visiting Charis and Hephaistos' illustrates an incident in the 'Iliad'.*

But no answer comes from any of the voices my soul flies to meet! My soul sickens at the courtesies that are showered on me. I sit at my countrymen's table like a dead man, sometimes yearning to be at sea and sometimes in the mountains, which divide you and ———— from me! My words flow like the last weary drops from a glass, and my eyes seek refuge in the dusk. O darkness, my light! What would become of Füssli now, if he had no nights!

Have you been to Baden since? Tell your friend there what I was unable to tell her and what I cannot well set down on paper either, for my spirit is as proud as her own. But if she is endowed with sympathies, she must already know more of me than you can tell her. Since I left, I have lain every night on the ground beside her bed – and when she became aware of me, a voice from her bed always asked me, 'What is my sister doing?' O, how I would answer that snuffling, prudish insult if only you were in my arms! And for your sake, you squinting eye of love – you rose – you lily – you creature of violets – you female virginity – you dear wringer of hands and cause of tears – for your sake, Italy and my native land are become foreign soil to me, and the spring sunshine turned to darkness. But go, and take some other – for I was once another's and perchance am so even yet.

But I am raving, for all this is frenzy for the peace of wedlock, and only *she*, the cause of my raving, to whom I do *not* write about it, can prefer it to common sense. But, dear Orell, either obtain permission for me to write to my beloved, or persuade *her* to write a word to *me* – and if it be as cold as the snow on Diana's bosom, for me it will be a consuming fire.

If you write to me, do please be circumstantial – that you may be as interesting as your friendship. Addio both!

Füssli

The 'she' of this letter was Anna Landolt, a niece of Lavater. She was wealthy and Fuseli, a poor painter, was not an acceptable suitor; her father sent him away. Some years later in London he married Sophia Rawlins, of Batheaston. Fuseli died in London in 1825.

This early painting by Trumbull of 'The Declaration of Independence' served as the model for one of his frescoes for the dome of the Capitol in Washington.

JOHN TRUMBULL TO THOMAS JEFFERSON

26 December 1816

Twenty eight years have elapsed, since under the kind protection of your hospitable roof at Chaillot, I painted your portrait in my picture of the Declaration of Independence, the composition of which had been planned two years before in your Library. The long period of War and Tumult which succeeded, palsied & suspended my work, and threw me as you know into other pursuits . . . The Government of the U.S. are restoring to more than their original Splender, the Buildings devoted to National purposes at Washington, which were barbarously sacrificed to the Rage of War. I have thought this a proper opportunity to make my first application for public patronage, and to request to be employed in decorating the walls of their buildings with the paintings which have employed so many [years] of my life . . . The Memory of your kindness & of the interest which you formerly took in this work is too strongly in my memory, to suffer a doubt to intrude of your

'The Surrender of General Burgoyne' recorded by Trumbull who had himself fought in the American War of Independence.

powerful protection at this time, – again, the work has been carried thus far by my own unaided exertions, *and can be finished only by me:* – future Artists may arise with far Superior Talents, but time has already withdrawn almost all their Models; and I who was one of the youngest Actors in the early scenes of the War, passed the Age of Sixty: – no time remains therefore for hesitation. Hoping that my application will meet your approbation, & support, & that you will honor me with an Answer addressed to me at Washington – Poste restante –

John Trumbull (1756–1843) was the chronicler of the American War of Independence. When it broke out he was an art-student; he joined the army and became one of Washington's officers; retiring with the rank of colonel in 1778. From 1780 to 1789 he lived in London, first studying under Benjamin West, then exhibiting frequently at the Royal Academy. The subjects of all his major works were patriotic. This application to Jefferson to do the big frescoes in the rebuilt Capitol at Washington was successful. As he points out he was uniquely well qualified for the job, having personally known and drawn or painted all the national leaders. The result is now part of the 'national mythology' of the United States.

RICHARD PARKES BONINGTON TO MADAME PERRIER AT
DUNKIRK
Paris, 31 December 1824

'Three days ago black went out of fashion and white came in; ostrich feathers are reappearing on the toques that win admiration at the 'Bouffons', and hang down to the ladies' shoulders to sustain an un-equal competition with white skin set off to advantage by the dresses, which are still in mourning [for Louis XVIII]. It must be confessed that owing to the economical spirit so decidedly prevalent this winter we still see some black taffeta hats, sparsely adorned with clusters of jet or with black flowers. But before the New Year brings its shower of comfits and sugar-plums to every chiffonier in our boudoirs, we shall no doubt be released from all this lugubrious apparel, and the approach of the month of March, with its joyous saturnalia, will be greeted by a complete change of costume.'

Reading these elegant phrases, you cannot but feel (as I do) extremely shocked at your compatriots. What! the whole of Paris is still in black, yet all the trappings of a more brilliant style of dress are already making their appearance, in the brightest and gayest colours! It seems to me that ostrich feathers would look as well on shoulders at Dunkirk as in Paris, and that collarettes or tippets of organdie or muslin will be more suitable by far. So I am sending you sketches of both. – I am also sending you everything I have been able to assemble in the way of toques, hats, berets, hats *à la trop cas d'Héro* [a play on the word Trocadéro] and so forth, all from the best milliner's workrooms in town.

Most of them have appeared at the 'Bouffes', which I have attended as a matter of course, but one would think oneself at a funeral ceremony rather than an Italian opera, with all the black toques, the crape and the gowns *à la missionnaire*; it takes some smiling faces and a Rossini overture to dispel the impression. Whereas at M. D——'s theatre one sees gowns of gauze and barège, figured ribbons, tulle mantles, flowers, blond-lace, etc., etc., etc.!

Ladies of Dunkirk, you are lost, or rather, your husbands are . . . a general resignation, no less. I offer you a charming prospect. Black! nothing but black!!!

M. Perrier will think me very ungrateful, but M. Poulain is pressing me to finish, I put him off to the last moment. Ask him to thank M. Morel d'Arras for remembering me. I will find a moment to scribble him a line. – Ladies, you must not hold it against me if I cross out words and make blots. For while I am writing to you someone comes in to ask me for some drawings, then the mending woman brings me some stockings, then comes the boot-black, then the bootmaker, I am furious but I must be pleasant this evening for I am dining out, always . . . luncheon . . .

I ventured to send you a few novels; I fear you will find them very insipid, but they are the fashion, the fashion! Colin begs you to accept the two enclosed drawings, I have a few lithographs by another of my friends.

This letter was written in French in reply to a request from Madame Perrier and her daughters for a description of the Paris fashions for the winter of 1824–1825.

Richard Parkes Bonington (1802–1828) was born in England but lived in France from the age of fifteen, his father having moved there in 1817 with the intention of setting up in the lace trade. He studied with Gros and was a friend of Delacroix and Géricault. A fluent draughtsman (Delacroix said of him that he was 'carried away by his own skill') his cliff landscapes and sea pictures were immediately successful, finding ready purchasers among the public. He paid visits to England in 1825 and 1827, and to Italy in 1826, and it was during a third visit to England in the autumn of 1828 that he died tragically young of tuberculosis.

'Paris. The Institute seen from the Quais' – a watercolour by the young English artist Richard Parkes Bonington who spent much of his short life in France.

GOTTFRIED SCHADOW TO BÖTTIGER

Berlin, 15 September 1802

For some time it has been in my mind, my honoured friend, to send you news of myself, and, as it were, to render you an account of my life as an artist. But writing calls for a special mood, and that visits us but seldom; the inclination, I would say, never at all; we artists have no inclination save for our own work; and if we are to write at all, we shall do better to wait until our thoughts have gathered into a flood that must burst out to relieve our hearts. You wish it, so I will tell you about myself.

The great part of my time is occupied with commissioned work, I seldom have an hour to give to my own whims; yet so many ideas come to mind which one would at least wish to capture with pencil on paper, and others to which one would like to give complete form!

I sometimes think of myself as a worthy craftsman, plying his trade in the town by carrying out his customers' orders. He has his workshop, his assistants and apprentices, and he will provide you with anything that falls within his own line of business. For neither I, my assistants nor my boys are clock-watchers, it is simply love of the work that brings us to it.

No; the only actual craftsmen among us are the stone-mason, the engraver, the polisher and the moulder; but the moulder has two different parts to play. He began life as a mason, then bettered himself by becoming a stucco-worker and after that, a man who wields hammer and chisel in obedience to strict mathematical precepts. He sets his plaster cast and his block of marble side by side, with a horizontal frame slung above and plumb-lines dangling over each of them at set distances; he measures the projections on the cast with a stick and cuts away the marble at the corresponding places, until his measuring-rod goes as far in from the plumb-line on the marble as from the corresponding one on the plaster model. We call this 'fixing points', or rather 'pointing a figure'. The distances between the points are marked by circles, so that the block of marble is scattered all over with little pencil dots, like the sky with stars, and not one of them must be further to left or right, or higher or lower, than it actually is. This work calls for unwavering concentration and a genuine love of precision. For sculpture on a flat background – in low or high relief – the procedure is different, and makes use of what is known as a 'crutch'; but I will say nothing of that, for mere description of such things cannot enable them to be visualized.

I have seldom been successful in conveying the idea of modelling and casting to a person who knows nothing of them; but even for the sake of the few one must make some attempt and it is worth while.

It may not add to the enjoyment of looking at a work of art, to know how it came into existence; but the artist's countrymen would surely hold him in affection and respect if they knew of the varied and irksome difficulties with which his mind and body must contend before a great work is brought to completion.

True, clay offers a soft pliable mass, lending itself to the removal or addition of pieces; but several years' practice is required before one can build standing figures and deal successfully with unsupported portions. Arms, hands, fingers and any other comparatively thin portions dry more quickly than the rest, and need either outward props or an inner framework of iron to keep them from collapsing. The clay model, once completed, is used to make a plaster cast, and the work thus changes from one material into another! Some people will ask 'Why?' The answer is that clay shrinks and becomes appreciably smaller, and that in a dry and unfired condition it is extremely brittle. A dry clay model could not be moved round very much, and would soon break when large calipers were used on it for measuring purposes; it might be fired, but if it is of any great size there will be no kiln to take it; it should be hollowed out and may shatter into a myriad pieces under the action of heat. For safety's sake, therefore, the transformation into plaster is adopted, though admittedly expensive. . . .

Before preparing the final model, one makes a smaller one, to preserve one's idea; often, of course, a sketch is needed as well, being easier to show to people or to send by letter; but it will not be much use to the sculptor, since it shows only *one* side, *one* aspect of the work.

If the statue is to be a clothed one, the clothes must be first arranged on a life-sized lay figure. Some garments may have to be put on it perhaps 20 times, before one is satisfied. Practice and experience are the best guides here. The model itself will be naked in the first place, and for good results there should be a living model to work from. . . . In Rome there are girls who earn their living by posing for artists; others, whether from bashfulness or because they are women, will offer only their head, throat, nape of the neck, arms and hands as models for studies. The German customs, climate and code of propriety combine to prevent this, and to open so many locks it is often necessary to resort to Jupiter's stratagem with Danaë. . . .

The working of marble needs many years' practice, and if a statue were to be made by only one worker it would exhaust anyone's patience; so the task is divided between three men, each with his own speciality. The first is the one already mentioned, who 'points' the work with the help of plumb-lines; this gives a rough-hewn shape, like a snowman. The second, a real artist, strips off the bark, as it were; the limbs of the figure are cut out and separated by him; he uses various types of drill for this purpose and for scooping out the deep folds in the clothing. The third, and most venturesome, is responsible for smoothing the skin, putting the last touches to the hair, giving final shape to the features – shaping the eyelids with the chisel is the most difficult operation here – finishing the hands and feet, and putting the final bloom on the whole work, which requires a sensitive touch even in polishing.

Johann Gottfried Schadow (1764–1850), the leading German classicist sculptor of the first half of the nineteenth century, studied in Rome from 1785 to 1787 and eventually, in 1816, became director of the Berlin Academy. His works include monuments, statues for tombs and portrait busts; his drawings and engravings are among the subtlest and liveliest records of the period.

'The working of marble needs many years' practice', *notes Schadow. Here he has portrayed Crown Princess Luise of Prussia and her sister Friedrike, who was later to become Queen of Hanover.*

PETER VON CORNELIUS TO FRIEDRICH FLEMMING

Düsseldorf

Ever since the spring my imagination has been wholly concentrated upon the idea of a speedy release from Düsseldorf. So you can easily imagine what an impression your letter made on me. Particularly as Vienna is exactly the place where I could progress towards my aim – viz., to make Raphael's style and composition more weighty, pleasing and attractive by combining them with Correggio's delightful gradation of shadows, while enlivening the colours through the use of Titian's vivid flesh-tints. Vienna is ideal for this purpose; the Gallery there possesses a great number of Titians and Correggios, whereas, as you know, we have only a few heads by those great men, not enough to judge them by. There are several fine pictures by Raphael there, too, so one can study him in every head. You can form a good idea of Correggio's beautiful shading when I tell you that Van der Werfft is studying it zealously but has not yet attained to it. Imagine a life-sized portrait in which light and shadow are treated in this way, with infinite gradations, but with clearer, purer tints in the shadows and bolder, more imaginative brushwork.

But the divine works of antiquity and mighty, everlasting nature must both stand by me constantly as tutelary spirits; for they are the dictionary of the language of art. If the artist translates the language of heart and imagination into the language of reality, he can always find in that book any words that may still be lacking in his vocabulary. I always laugh at myself when I begin chattering about art, for I become as voluble as a ladies' milliner. But we all have our weak point, as you and Jonay say, and that is what we defend most vigorously.

Nowadays I often reflect upon myself and my situation, and come to the conclusion – I am now discussing the most important point with a man like Plato, who will not dismiss the candid words of his Raphael as boastful vanity – and come, after searching my conscience, to the conclusion that I am capable of carrying art to a pretty high level. But that means I ought now to give my whole time to art; the noblest products of ancient and modern art should now form the pattern of my daily life; my best ideas should no longer be smothered at birth by unworthy toil

'I . . . come, after searching my conscience, to the conclusion that I am capable of carrying art to a pretty high level' – *a detail from Cornelius' fresco of 'The Last Judgment' in the Ludwigskirche in Munich.*

that blunts the artistic spirit. The spirit should be able to soar boldly in magnificent flight, its pinions no longer dragged down by leaden weights. The artist must be left free and unfettered to wing with all haste away from this petty world, into the boundless realms of art!

Peter von Cornelius (1783–1867), a native of Düsseldorf, lived in Rome from 1811 to 1819. He was a leading member of the 'Nazarene' school, a brotherhood of painters whose aim was to bring piety back into art, who led a communal life and took Raphael as their model. Cornelius outgrew this movement and developed into a 'history painter' on the grand scale. (His 'Last Judgment' in the Ludwigskirche, Munich, is bigger than Michelangelo's.) He is important as a teacher and administrator, first in Munich and later in Berlin.

29

PHILIPP OTTO RUNGE TO JOHANN WOLFGANG VON GOETHE

Wolgast, 3 July 1806

After a short walking-tour round our charming island of Rügen, where the quiet solemnity of the sea is interrupted in a variety of ways by friendly promontories and valleys, hills and cliffs, I returned home to find not only an affectionate welcome from my family, but your esteemed letter as well; and it is a great relief to me to see the fulfilment of my dearest wish, that my work might afford you some degree of pleasure. I am very sensible of your approval of efforts which do not take the direction you wish art to follow; and it would be foolish to give you my reasons for working as I do, or to attempt to convince you that they are the right ones.

Practice is attended by great difficulties for everyone, but particularly, in our day, for one who sets out as a beginner at an age when reason has already gained a considerable hold over him; he will court disaster if he tries to sink his own personality in a general, single effort. He who loses himself in the infinite complexity of the life around him and is thus irresistibly impelled to portray it, feels himself powerfully stirred by the total impression, and feels exactly like this either when he penetrates the characteristics of each detail or when he seeks to penetrate the relationships between nature and the great masses. He who observes the great masses with a constant sense that everything, down to the smallest detail, is lively and exerts an influence on everything else, cannot think of them without perceiving a special connection or relationship between them; much less can he represent them without reference to basic causes.

To put it more clearly, I believe that had the early German artists had some knowledge of form, they would have lost the direct, natural expression of their figures until they had reached a certain proficiency in that study. It has often happened that a man has built bridges and arches and very ingenious things in an absolutely impromptu manner. That may be all very well for a time; but when he reaches a certain stage of development at which he stumbles upon mathematical conclusions, all his talent deserts him unless he can work his way back to freedom through science. Thus, since I first began to puzzle over the particular phenomena produced by mixing the primary colours, I knew no peace until I had formed a certain picture of the whole world of colour, comprehensive enough to include all transformations and phenomena.

It is perfectly natural for a painter looking at a beautiful landscape or hearing some discussion of an effect to be seen in nature, to desire to know what combination of materials can reproduce that effect. At all events that was what prompted me to study the individual qualities of colours and try to discover whether it were possible so far to penetrate their power as to discern what they can do, or what can be done by their means, and what affects them. I hope you will look indulgently upon this attempt to explain to you in writing, views that I think can in fact only be fully demonstrated in practice. Lastly, I think it is not only useful but even indispensable for painters to study colour from this angle; and the effort to gain some complete visual understanding of colours is neither impeded nor rendered superfluous by this approach.

A firm belief that there is a definite spiritual connection between the elements may finally bring the painter a consolation and cheerfulness to which he cannot attain by any other means, for thus his individual existence is swallowed up in his work and the fusion of materials, medium, and purpose finally creates in him a fullness which, since it can be maintained only by continual zealous and faithful striving, must also have some beneficial effect upon others.

When I consider the materials with which I work and measure them by the standard of these qualities, I perceive with certainty where and

'I believe . . . I could get much further if I had sufficient knowledge of chemistry and mathematics. I hope with all my heart that I may have the opportunity to acquire that knowledge.' *Runge was to die four years later, however, at the age of only thirty-three. He painted this self-portrait in the year of his death.*

how I can employ them, for no material with which we work is absolutely pure. I cannot go into details of practice here, firstly because it would take too long and secondly because all I had in mind was to show you from what point of view I look at colour; and I readily admit that much of this is still very lame. I believe, too, that my pursuit of this path has not been quite without profit for others, though I could get much further if I had sufficient knowledge of chemistry and mathematics. I hope with all my heart that I may have the opportunity to acquire that knowledge.

Philipp Otto Runge (1777–1810) is, with Caspar David Friedrich, the most important representative of the Romantic movement in Germany. He first painted vigorous portraits, turning later to mystical, religious visions ('The Hours of the Day') full of nature-symbolism. Towards the end of his short life, he took up the scientific study of colour, and this brought him into correspondence with Goethe, whose 'Farbenlehre' was an attempt to formulate a theory of colour in opposition to Newtonian optics and based more on sensation than measurement.

Two of Runge's sketches for 'The Hours of the Day': (left) 'The Lily of Light' – a study for the larger version of 'Morning', and (right) 'Noon'.

CASPAR DAVID FRIEDRICH IN SOME 'THOUGHTS ON ART'

X is also one of the many present-day painters whose studies, drawn or painted from nature, are quite admirable; but when they come to be used for pictures, so that the original scene is no longer present to the painter's physical eyes and he has to rely on his spiritual eyes, every recognizable trace of the earlier studies is lost. Whereas many other painters are timid and awkward in drawing from nature, but when it comes to using their sketches for pictures, the whole thing comes to life.

The artist's feeling is his law. Genuine feeling can never be contrary to nature, it is always in harmony with her. But another person's feelings should never be imposed on us as law. Spiritual affinity leads to similarity in work, but such affinity is something entirely different from mimicry. Whatever people may say of Y's paintings and how they often resemble Z's, yet they proceed from Y and are his sole property.

People say of such-and-such a painter that he has great command of his brush. Might it not be more correct to say that he is controlled by his brush? Merely for the satisfaction of his vanity, to paint brilliantly and display skill with the brush, he has sacrificed the nobler considerations of naturalness and truth – and thus achieved sorry fame as a brilliant technician.

Two halves make a whole, but anyone who is half a musician and half a painter is only a complete half. There can be complete quarters in the same way, and even smaller fractions – our schools appear to be aiming at this.

In this big moonlit landscape by the painter N.N., that deservedly celebrated technician, one sees more than one would wish, or than can actually be seen by moonlight. But what the perceptive, sensitive soul looks for in every picture, and rightly expects to find, is missing from this as from all paintings by N.N. If that painter could find it in himself to paint fewer, but more deeply-felt, pictures instead of so many clever ones, his contemporaries and posterity would be more grateful to him.

People are always talking about 'incidentals'; but nothing is incidental in a picture, everything is indispensable to the whole effect, so nothing must be neglected. If a man can give value to the main part of his composition only by negligent treatment of the subordinate portions, his work is in a bad way. Everything must and can be carefully executed, without the different parts obtruding themselves on the eye. The proper subordination of the parts to the whole is not achieved by neglecting incidental features, but by correct grouping and by the distribution of light and shadow.

Caspar David Friedrich (1774–1840) was one of the masters of the German Romantic movement. He combined a meticulous technique in the rendering of landscape – particularly wild forests and mountain scenes – with a religious feeling that everything in nature should be 'represented as an expression of the divine presence'. He spent most of his life in Dresden.

A winter landscape, dark forests and Gothic towers – a picture that draws on three of the most potent sources of Romanticism: truth to reality, a sense of the sublime in nature, and an emotional regard for medieval Christianity. Caspar David Friedrich's 'The Cross and the Cathedral in the Mountains' was painted in 1811.

'The Thames near Walton Bridge' – an early landscape by Turner which was probably painted out-of-doors.

J. M. W. TURNER TO THE REV. HENRY TRIMMER

47 Queen Anne Street, London
1 August 1815

My dear Sir,
I lament that all hope of the pleasure of seeing you, or getting to Heston, must for the present probably vanish. My father told me on Saturday last, when I was, as usual, compelled to return to town the same day, that you and Mrs Trimmer would leave Heston for Suffolk as to-morrow, Wednesday. In the first place, I am glad to hear that her health is so far established as to be equal to the journey, and to give me your utmost hope for her benefiting by the sea air being fully realised; 'twill give me great pleasure to hear, and the earlier the better.

After next Tuesday, if you have a moment's time to spare, a line will reach me at Farnley Hall, near Otley, Yorkshire, and for some time, as Mr Fawkes talks of keeping me in the North by a trip to the Lakes, and until November. Therefore I suspect I am not to see Sandycombe. Sandycombe sounds just now in my ears as an act of folly, when I reflect how little I have been able to be there this year, and less chance (perhaps) for the next. In looking forward to a Continental excursion, and poor

35

Daddy seems as much plagued with weeds as I am with disappointment – that if Miss —— would but waive bashfulness, or, in other words, make an offer instead of expecting one, the same might change occupiers; but not to trouble you further, allow me, with most sincere respect to Mrs Trimmer and family, to consider myself

Yours most truly obliged,

J. M. W. Turner

This is one of the few letters dealing with the artist's private life. The lady concerned was a relation of the Rev. Trimmer of Southwold, Suffolk. Turner did not dare to propose, and remained a bachelor to the end.

Turner was born in 1775, the son of a barber. At the age of fourteen he was apprenticed to a London architect and worked for a time as a draughtsman and magazine illustrator. His subsequent extensive travels led to the publication of volumes of views of Scotland, Switzerland and Italy; taking Claude Lorrain as his model, he turned to large landscapes; and his final period is marked by the great colour-fantasies that seem like the forerunners in painting of Wagner's 'endless melody'.

Turner had a dual personality, combining a shrewd business sense, which earned him a fortune, with a reserve carried to the point of secretiveness and he ended by leading a double life in the literal sense, in two different houses. His brightest and most colourful pictures were painted in dark, dusty rooms and John Ruskin, his earliest champion, found that a great part of the enormous body of work he left behind him was mouldy and half spoilt by damp. One result of Turner's morbid obsession with privacy was that he left very little written evidence behind him.

J. M. W. TURNER TO HIS FRIEND GEORGE JONES, R.A.

London, February 1830

Dear Jones,

I delayed answering yours until the chance of this finding you in Rome, to give you some account of the dismal prospect of Academic affairs, and of the last sad ceremonies paid yesterday to departed talent gone to that bourne from whence no traveller returns. Alas! only two short months

Sir Thomas [Lawrence] followed the coffin of Dawe to the same place. We then were his pall-bearers. Who will do the like for me, or when, God only knows how soon. My poor father's death proved a heavy blow upon me, and has been followed by others of the same dark kind. However, it is something to feel that gifted talent can be acknowledged by the many who yesterday waded up to their knees in snow and muck to see the funeral pomp swelled up by carriages of the great, without the persons themselves. *Entre nous,* much could be written on this subject; much has been in the papers daily of anecdotes, sayings and doings, contradictory and complex, and nothing certain, excepting that a great mass of property in the unfinished pictures will cover more than demands. The portraits of the potentates are to be exhibited, which will of course produce a large sum. The drawings of the old masters are to be offered to his Majesty in mass, then to the British Museum. Thomas Campbell is to write Sir Thomas's life at the request of the family, and a portrait of himself, painted lately and engraved, for which great biddings have been already made. I wish I had you by the button-hole, notwithstanding all your grumbling about Italy and yellow. I could then tell more freely what has occurred since your departure of combinations and concatenations somewhat of the old kind, only more highly coloured, and to my jaundiced eye not a whit more pure. . . . Chantrey is as gay and as good as ever, ready to serve: he requests, for my benefit, that you bottle up all the yellows which may be found straying out of the right way; but what you may have told him about the old masters which you did not tell me, I can't tell, but we expected to hear a great deal from each other, but the stormy brush of Tintoretto was only to make 'the Notte' more visible. May you be better in health and spirits.

Adieu, adieu; faithfully yours,

J. M. W. Turner

George Dawe had died in 1829, Sir Thomas Lawrence on 7 January 1830. 'The portraits of the potentates' were Lawrence's series of portraits of all the allied sovereigns at the Congress of Aix-la-Chapelle in 1818, and 'The drawings of the old masters' his incomparable collection of drawings by Raphael, Michelangelo,

Turner's unfinished 'Rocky Bay with Classic Figures' was painted at the time of his second visit to Italy in 1828. His paintings of this period were criticized for their yellow tone.

Leonardo and others. 'Italy and yellow' refers to the mustard tone of Turner's later Italian pictures, which Jones and the sculptor Chantrey had teased him about.

Turner was not a great letter writer. He had difficulties in expressing himself in writing, and even verbally. In addition, his extreme sensitiveness regarding all personal matters, and also his art, prevented him from giving any substantial account of his views on his life or work. He even painted behind locked doors if he was at a stranger's house, or covered his drawing if anyone approached him.

The letter to the father of a young aspiring painter, James Astbury Hammersley, is one of the few instances when he said a word about his profession:

J. M. W. TURNER TO JOHN HAMMERSLEY

47 Queen Anne Street, London
4 December 1848

Dear Sir,

I have truly, I must say, written three times, and I now hesitate; for did I know your son's works, or, as you say, *gifted merit*, yet even then I would rather advise you to think well, and not be carried away by the admiration which any friendly hopes (which ardent friends to early talent) may assume: they know not the difficulties or the necessities of the culture of the *Fine Arts*, generally speaking. In regard to yourself, it is you alone can judge how far you are inclined to support him during perhaps a long period of expense; and particularly if you look towards tuition, the more so; for it cannot insure success (however much it may facilitate practice), and therefore it behoves you to weigh well the means in your power before you embark in a profession which requires more care, assiduity and perseverance than any person can guarantee.

I have the honour to be,
Your humble Servant, J. M. W. Turner

'*A Venetian Scene. St Benedetto looking towards Fusina*' – Turner's three brief visits to Venice inspired a number of paintings.

JOHN CONSTABLE TO THE REV. JOHN FISHER

East Bergholt, 22 June 1812

From the window where I am now writing, I see all those sweet fields where we have passed so many happy hours together. I called at the Rectory on Saturday with my mother. The doctor was unusually courteous, and shook hands with me on taking leave. Am I to argue from this that I am not *entirely* out of the pale of salvation? How delighted I am that you are fond of Cowper. But how could it be otherwise? for he is the poet of religion and nature. I think the world much indebted to Mr Hayley. I never saw, till now, the supplement to the letters; perhaps some of his best are to be found there, and it contains an interesting account of the death of poor Rose, a young friend of the poet's. Nothing can exceed the beautiful appearance of the country; its freshness, its amenity.

'Mr Hayley' is Blake's friend William Hayley, whose 'Life of Cowper' had appeared in 1803–1804.

Unlike Turner, Constable was particularly fluent in expressing himself on paper. Like Rembrandt he was the son of a miller. He was born in 1776 in the rural county of Suffolk and became the greatest English landscape painter of the nineteenth century. A traditionalist, he had great faith in theories and teachers, particularly Claude Lorrain and the Dutch painters; but he could also shake off the influence of studios and schools:

When I sit down to make a sketch from nature, the first thing I try to do is to forget that I have ever seen a picture.

This most English of painters, who never left his native island and found the subjects of his greatest pictures in his own surroundings, was unnoticed in England during his lifetime except by a few friends and connoisseurs. But he had a considerable influence on French painting, and the exhibition of his 'Hay Wain' in Paris in 1824 was an epoch-making event.

Constable disliked everything that smacked of literature, though he gave lectures on 'Landscape Art' in 1833 and 1836; his real journals and self-revelations are his sketches from nature.

JOHN CONSTABLE TO THE REV. JOHN FISHER

22 July 1812

I have been living a hermit-like life, though always with my pencil in my hand. Perhaps this has not been much the case with hermits, if we except Swaneveldt (the pupil of Claude); who was called the 'Hermit of Italy', from the romantic solitudes he lived in, and which his pictures so admirably describe. How much real delight have I had with the study of landscape this summer! either I am myself improved in the art of seeing nature, which Sir Joshua calls painting, or nature has unveiled her beauties to me less fastidiously. Perhaps there is something of both, so we will divide the compliment. But I am writing this nonsense with a sad heart, when I think what would be my happiness could I have this enjoyment with you. Then indeed would my mind be calm to contemplate the endless beauties of this happy country.

JOHN CONSTABLE TO THE REV. JOHN FISHER

Hampstead, 23 October 1821

My dear Fisher,

. . . I am most anxious to get into my London painting-room, for I do not consider myself at work unless I am before a six-foot canvas. I have done a good deal of skying, for I am determined to conquer all difficulties, and that among the rest. And now talking of skies, it is amusing to us to see how admirably you fight my battles; you certainly take the best possible ground for getting your friend out of a scrape (the example of the old masters). That landscape painter who does not make his skies a very material part of his composition, neglects to avail himself of one of his greatest aids. Sir Joshua Reynolds, speaking of the landscapes of Titian, of Salvator, and of Claude, says: 'Even their *skies* seem to sympathize with their subjects.' I have often been advised to consider my sky as '*a white sheet* thrown behind the objects'. Certainly, if the sky is obtrusive, as mine are, it is bad; but if it is evaded, as mine are not, it is worse; it must and always shall with me make an effectual part of the

'That landscape painter who does not make his skies a very material part of his composition, neglects to avail himself of one of his greatest aids.' *Constable did this painting of Weymouth Bay in 1816.*

composition. It will be difficult to name a class of landscape in which the sky is not the key note, the standard of scale, and the chief organ of sentiment. You may conceive, then, what a 'white sheet' would do for me, impressed as I am with these notions, and they cannot be erroneous. The sky is the source of light in nature, and governs everything; even our common observations on the weather of every day are altogether suggested by it. The difficulty of skies in painting is very great, both as to composition and execution; because, with all their brilliancy, they ought not to come forward, or, indeed, be hardly thought of any more than extreme distances are; but this does not apply to phenomena or accidental effects of sky, because they always attract particularly. I may say all this

42

'. . . I associate "my careless boyhood" with all that lies on the banks of the Stour; those scenes made me a painter' – *a favourite subject was Dedham Mill. This sketch dates from about 1819.*

to you, though *you* do not want to be told that I know very well what I am about, and that my skies have not been neglected, though they have often failed in execution, no doubt, from an over-anxiety about them, which will alone destroy that easy appearance which nature always has in all her movements.

How much I wish I had been with you on your fishing excursion in the New Forest! What river can it be? But the sound of water escaping from mill-dams, &c., willows, old rotten planks, slimy posts, and brick-work, I love such things. Shakespeare could make everything poetical; he tells us of poor Tom's haunts among 'sheep cotes and mills'. As long as I do paint, I shall never cease to paint such places. They have always

43

been my delight, and I should indeed have been delighted in seeing what you describe, and in your company, 'in the company of a man to whom nature does not spread her volume in vain'. Still I should paint my own places best; painting is with me but another word for feeling, and I associate 'my careless boyhood' with all that lies on the banks of the Stour; those scenes made me a painter, and I am grateful; that is, I had often thought of pictures of them before I ever touched a pencil, and your picture is the strongest instance of it I can recollect; but I will say no more, for I am a great egotist in whatever relates to painting. Does not the Cathedral look beautiful among the golden foliage? its solitary grey must sparkle in it.

'Salisbury Cathedral from the Bishop's Garden.' It was on the invitation of the Bishop, whom he had met in Suffolk and London, that Constable went to Salisbury for the first time in the autumn of 1811, and it was on this same occasion that he first met the Bishop's nephew, John Fisher, who was to become one of his greatest friends. This picture, one of a number done by Constable of the Cathedral and its precincts, was painted for Fisher in 1826.

JOHN CONSTABLE TO C. R. LESLIE, R.A.

2 April 1833

Do not pass my door if you come to town. I have brushed up my 'Cottage' into a pretty look, and my 'Heath' is almost safe, but I must stand or fall by my 'House'. I had on Friday a long visit from Mr —— alone; but my pictures do not come into his rules or whims of the art, and he said I had 'lost my way'. I told him that I had, 'perhaps, other notions of art than picture admirers have in general. I looked on pictures as *things to be avoided,* connoisseurs looked on them as things to be *imitated*; and that, too, with such a deference and humbleness of submission, amounting to a total prostration of mind and original feeling, as must serve only to fill the world with abortions.' But he was very agreeable, and endured the visit, I trust, without the usual courtesies of life being violated. What a sad thing it is that this lovely art is so wrested to its own destruction! Used only to blind our eyes, and to prevent us from seeing the sun shine – the fields bloom – the trees blossom – and from hearing the foliage rustle; while old black rubbed out and dirty canvases take the place of God's own works. I long to see you. I love to cope with you, like Jacques, in my 'sullen moods', for I am not fit for the present world of art . . . Lady Morley was here yesterday. On seeing the 'House' she exclaimed, 'How fresh, how dewy, how exhilarating!' I told her half of this, if I could think I deserved it, was worth all the talk and cant about pictures in the world.

JOHN CONSTABLE TO GEORGE CONSTABLE

Well Walk, Hampstead
20 December 1833

My dear friend,
I thank you most sincerely for your kind and friendly letter. I am sadly out of order, but you seem determined that I shall not knock under. I am too unwell to go to town, but my friend Bonner has just set off to Charlotte Street to pack your picture and forward it; it is a beautiful representation of a summer's evening; calm, warm and delicious; the colour on the man's face is perfect sunshine. The liquid pencil of this

school is replete with a beauty peculiar to itself. Nevertheless, I don't believe they had any *nostrums*, but plain linseed oil; '*honest linseed*', as old Wilson called it. But it is always right to remember that the ordinary painters of that day used, as now, the same vehicle as their betters, and also that their works have all received the hardening and enamelling effects of time, so that we must not judge of originality by these signs always. Still your picture has a beautiful look; but I shall not collect any more. I have sent most of my *old men* to Mr Davidson's Gallery in Pall Mall to be sold. I find my house too much encumbered with lumber, and this encumbers my mind. My sons are returned from Folkestone for Christmas. John is delighted with the collection [of fossils] you have sent him; he says they are very valuable indeed, and he highly prizes them. To me these pieces of 'time-mangled matter' are interesting for the tale they tell; but above all, I esteem them as marks of regard to my darling boy, the darling, too, of his dear mother.

'The Marine Parade and Chain Pier, Brighton.' Though Constable disliked Brighton, 'The genteeler part, the marine parade, is still more unnatural – with its trimmed and neat appearance . . .', *it nevertheless became the subject of one of his most outstanding sky-studies in this painting which dates from 1824.*

THE MID-NINETEENTH CENTURY

JEAN AUGUSTE DOMINIQUE INGRES TO HIS FRIEND
M. VARCOLLIER

Rome, 31 August 1840

My dear Varcollier,
I should feel myself too privileged if, at a distance of four hundred
leagues, I could bare my heart to you; you would see in it the lively,
tender friendship I have always had for you and yours. Believe me, in
spite of my detestable negligence, nothing can change that true affection;
it goes too far back for that.

How touched I am by what you tell me about our mutual friends,
their flattering impatience for my return, and the kindness with which
they think of me. I do what I can to be worthy of so much praise; but
shall I ever deserve the unduly high esteem in which you hold me? I must
accept such tributes only in a spirit of emulation, with the same feeling
that stirs in me at the sight of the masterpieces before which I do
obeisance here, trying to imitate them, but, alas, from such a distance!

You have probably seen my little picture of 'Stratonice'. It is not for
me to speak of it, except perhaps to mention the infinite trouble it cost
me. It would give me great happiness, dear friend, to learn that it has the
good fortune to please you and my dear pupil and friend Madame
Varcollier, whom I embrace from here with all my heart, while
awaiting the resumption of our pleasant little musical evenings. That
reminds me of our worthy, respectable and eminent Baillot, whom I
shall be so delighted to see again, like others among our friends, whom
I have not forgotten; please be sure to tell them so.

You speak in such good terms of M. Reber that I must needs think
very highly of him, having known so long how closely our tastes agree.
Ah! my dear friend, in that respect I shall return to you just as I went
away, putting Raphael above all others because his divine grace is
accompanied by precisely the right degree of character and strength,
never exceeding the measure. Whom can one rank beside him? No one,
unless it be he who in music has the same soul, my divine Mozart; both
of them wise and great as God himself! But while I bow before their
altars I do not neglect to worship many others for whom you, I know,

feel the same devotion – I mean Gluck, Beethoven and that charming Haydn, whose pages we will leaf through again when I am back in Paris.

I so much enjoy giving free rein to my pen on subjects of which I know you are as fond as I am, that it brings tears to my eyes, and makes

'The Madonna del Gran Duca'
– a drawing after Raphael's
famous painting of about 1505
in the Pitti Palace, Florence.

me tremble with a happiness I cannot describe. And my wife says I shall soon be sixty years old! That is possible, but never did I feel so young in spirit. No, never have I felt more love of that beauty which makes one so happy, so glad to be alive, even in this pestiferous world; for contact with the world cannot rob us, the privileged few, of the joys of sympathetic communication, the secret delight that comes from love of art . . .

It seems you are doing wonders at the Hôtel de Ville. After archi-tecture it will, I hope, be the turn of sculpture and painting, especially of fresco; do not you agree?

I am relying on you for when I get back, to make up our party of four with Defresne and Paul Delaroche and hear again at the Conservatoire the symphonies of the great, the thrilling, the inimitable Beethoven. We shall meet soon. I embrace you.

J. Ingres

'You have probably seen my little picture of "Stratonice". It is not for me to speak of it, except perhaps to mention the infinite trouble it cost me.' *Ingres had in fact been working on this painting of 'Antiochus and Stratonice' for four years. One of a number of versions of the same subject, the picture now hangs in the Musée Condé, Chantilly.*

Commissioned as a ceiling decoration for a room in the Louvre, 'The Apotheosis of Homer' was painted in 1827.

This letter, written from Rome where Ingres had been living as director of the École de Rome since 1834, reflects the passions that had swayed him all his life – his love of music, his delight in society, his concern for the moral grandeur of art. In music Ingres seems to have placed Mozart and Gluck highest of all – at least they are the only two composers included in his large painting of 'The Apotheosis of Homer' which he regarded as his artistic testament. The 'Stratonice', begun in 1836, was only completed in 1840. Most of his works cost Ingres 'infinite trouble', and he left many of them unfinished.

  Jean Auguste Dominique Ingres (1780–1867) was born at Montauban and studied under David in Paris. He had a hard struggle for recognition, even though he won the Prix de Rome at an early age; for nearly twenty years he lived in Italy as an obscure portrait painter, turning out travellers' portraits at two guineas apiece. Not until 1824, when he was forty-four, was he recognized, by the award of an official commission, as a master and 'chef d'école'.

JEAN AUGUSTE DOMINIQUE INGRES TO HIS FRIEND
M. MARCOTTE

Dampierre, 8 August 1847

One could almost count the days when we see each other in Paris, and that is not how a man should live with his friends; but it is this painting which, in return for but little, or, if you prefer, for too much, enjoyment, robs me of so much of the time I ought to devote to friendship by living at last like a human being, as one should. That cruel *tyrant* even prevents me from sleeping, such is her determination to reign alone, in undivided authority, and you should see how she sets about it at Dampierre! In the first place she will not allow me to take even the shortest walk, so much as a turn round the château – or very rarely. The moment I rise – to work! Get your things ready and go off until noon. Then I am graciously allowed to take a glance at the newspaper; then, just before two o'clock, she drives me away to the gallery until eight o'clock in the evening, without stirring. I arrive for dinner, tired out . . . Yet I love her, the wretch, and passionately, still; for when all's said and done she loves me too, and if I did not return her devotion she would threaten me with weakness, with decrepitude in my work, with desertion, even death. And thus it is that, after many struggles and with unabated courage, one is not too conscious of being on the wrong side of sixty-seven . . . Anyhow, I am in form; all goes well, well enough and quickly enough, and if I make as good use of my remaining two and a half months as I have of my time up to now, I may hope to have finished this 'Golden Age' by next year, God willing!

Ingres had undertaken to decorate the walls of the great hall of the Château de Dampierre for the Duc de Luynes with two large wall-paintings – 'The Golden Age' and 'The Iron Age'; he worked at the former for several years without being able to finish it. The literary context of his pictures was always of extreme importance to him. He was a considerable theorist, upholding and defending his 'doctrine' constantly before pupils and critics. Some of his remarks seemed contradictory: one day he would say, 'You must note that only curved lines are to be found in nature', and another, 'The straight line predominates in nature – those

A detail from Ingres' wall-painting, 'The Golden Age', at the Château de Dampierre. It was never completed.

great beautiful straight lines!' He was fond of referring to Apelles, who said that the artist should not let a day pass without drawing a line; for, he explained, 'line is drawing, and that is the whole of our art'.

JEAN AUGUSTE DOMINIQUE INGRES' ADVICE ON ART
GIVEN TO HIS PUPILS
1864

If I could make musicians of you all, it would be to your advantage as painters. All is harmony in nature, a little too much, or a little less, disturbs the scale and strikes a discordant note. One has to learn to sing true with the pencil or brush, just as with the voice; correct form is like correct sound.

In drawing, let your style be pure, but bold. Pure and bold – that is drawing, that is art.

Have a religious feeling for your art. Do not suppose that anything good, or even fairly good, can be produced without nobility of soul. To become accustomed to beauty, fix your eyes on the sublime. Look neither to right nor left, much less downwards. Go forward with your head raised towards the skies, instead of bent towards the ground, like pigs routing in the mud.

I am a man of my country, a Gaul, but not of those who sacked Rome and tried to burn Delphi. There are still such among you. True, they no longer wreak destruction by force of arms; but in their petty pride and the disorder of their shabby notions, these little present-day Gauls direct their efforts against their own country, working to deprive it of its real art. They undermine the roots of that art; like termites, they gnaw away its marrow until at last it falls and crumbles into dust. Some people may find me harsh and severe, but desperate ills calls for desperate remedies. Besides, I believe I do not exceed the bounds of justice in my steadfast opinions and in a sincere love of art which no one, at least, will venture to question. . . Let them think me singular, intolerant, eccentric; as my lofty tastes are part of a religion, as I can justify the nobility of what I love and adore, it will be understood, not to mention the sensitiveness of my nerves, whence come my so-called eccentricities and why I am intolerant!

Hippolyte Flandrin, the favourite pupil of Ingres, and his brother Paul, who was also an artist, in a double portrait dating from 1835.

HIPPOLYTE FLANDRIN ON THE PROJECTED REORGANIZA‑ TION OF THE ÉCOLE DES BEAUX‑ARTS

Rome, December 1863

They want to set up a School, they want to teach, while entirely re‑ jecting tradition, as though teaching and tradition were not synonymous! They exercise their minds about originality, as though originality could be handed on! Originality cannot be taught, but a School offers it an opportunity to develop by giving body and form to the propensities of the mind . . . You speak of freedom, of freedom of instruction! I tell you there is an age at which to learn and an age at which to judge, to choose. Only at that age can there be any question of freedom, the freedom which causes you so much reflection. I maintain that in an Art School, as in any other, it is the duty of the government to teach only truths which are unquestioned, or which are at least supported by the finest examples and accepted from century to century. Once they leave the School, the pupils will shape these noble traditions into the truth of their own day, of that you may be confident; a genuine truth, for it will be the product of true freedom, whereas to teach the pros and cons, in the same place and, so to speak, out of the same mouths, can only produce doubt and discouragement . . . No, it is not doubt that teaches, it is affirmation, and that is why I did not want to take part in a kind of teaching which is without principles and without faith. Since I am fortunate enough to believe, I do not want to say: 'Here is something that may be beautiful', but I want to say: 'Here is something that is beautiful', without a Council, higher or no, to come blowing now hot, now cold and destroying my work . . . The first and best method of teaching, to my mind, is to promote respect and reverence for beautiful things, proclaiming them as the most beautiful by the position in which we set them, the care we devote to them. In short, say in every way possible: 'This is what one must love, honour, admire.'

Hippolyte Flandrin (1809–1864) was the favourite pupil of Ingres and, as these notes show, the staunchest of traditionalists. On 15 November, M. de Nieuwerkerke, the superintendent of the Beaux-Arts, had published a report in which he proposed a number of reforms for the reorganization of the École des Beaux-Arts – the autonomy of the school was to be suppressed, subjects other than art, but which had some bearing on it, such as costume, the latest scientific discoveries on paint, etc., could be taught there by people from outside the school who would also be free to present any new theories they might have about art, and the Rome scholarships were to be cut from five to two years. Flandrin was notified by the Ministry that his appointment as a professor at the school had ceased but that he had been appointed by the government as a 'chef d'atelier' in the new organization. He refused the post, however, as he opposed the reforms. His notes towards a work discussing the reorganization of the school were never completed as Ingres published his own 'Réponse' first.

Flandrin's main works were large religious and classical compositions, and murals for the redecoration of the medieval churches then being 'restored' as a result of the religious revival of that day, but he also painted some of the finest portraits of his generation.

PAUL GAVARNI IN A NOTE FOUND AMONGST HIS PAPERS

When I was a very little boy they made me draw eyes in profile, with charcoal: I found it very tedious; I did four without understanding what it was all about, and that was all, the teacher went away; I filled three exercise-books with horsemen, brigands, houses with smoke, pictures of the chevalier Bayard, little dogs, and little boys tugging at kites; afterwards I did some Cossacks, when I had seen some. Later on came the iron gate of the Bulet boarding-school with its two cannon-balls, and M. Magest's balloon, and if I had not used them all up for paper dolls or crackers, I would make a handsome gilt-edged book out of them.

Both the enthusiasm and the subjects that aroused it are charmingly characteristic of the artist who was to become the most popular and prolific graphic artist in Paris. Gavarni, whose real name was Sulpice Guillaume Chevalier, was born in 1804 and began his career as an illustrator of fashion magazines. He was soon flourishing as a pictorial chronicler of Parisian life, working for illustrated magazines and publishing volumes of engravings with witty, satirical captions showing a gift for epigram equal to his power of graphic expression.

PAUL GAVARNI IN HIS DIARY

Paris, 20 November 1828

How empty or worn-out one must be, to feel bored in a great centre of population! You there, stick your nose out of your attic window; see that multitude of roofs, with the smoke rising from them! Blow out your lamp, put on your breeches and slip out for half a day among the host of interests that compose the mud in the streets, go in to right or left, wipe your boots on the drawing-room carpet, have a drink at the bar, warm yourself at the forge, go and watch a thief being tried or a law being passed, venture some gold on the turn of a roulette wheel, or buy and sell under the pillars of a market, you will come home full of pictures . . . Whenever I return from a visit to Paris I feel convinced that it still waits to be described, and am tormented by the longing to try.

Every time, at every step, I find many things there, and to count the feelings that come to me there in a day, I should need a year.

PAUL GAVARNI'S PREFACE FOR THE 'JOURNAL DES GENS DU MONDE'

Paris, November 1833

Look, gentlemen; look, ladies! Here is Paris, the capital! Paris, the beautiful! Paris, the city of wits! Paris, the city of good manners! Paris, the city where people know how to walk, to bow, to smile, to fail, to do everything in the right style! Here is Paris. Look! look, you from the provinces; look, you from across the sea; look, Germans; look, Russians; look, from wherever you come, you who would learn to wear a hat, to use scent, to introduce yourselves; you who wish to speak well, laugh well, see well, live well, here is Paris!

The voices of Paris!
The eyes of Paris!
The words of Paris!
The tunes of Paris!
The balls of Paris!
The hats of Paris!
The ribbons of Paris!
The smells of Paris!
The raillery of Paris!
All the nothings of Paris! Paris, Paris, here is Paris.

PAUL GAVARNI TO A FRIEND

Paris, Wednesday evening, c. 1838

My dear fellow,

In paintings and books, people always see themselves too much in perspective, like the little houses in landscapes. It is true the soul and the heart are sometimes mentioned, but in a vague, obscure fashion. – Or else those objects are studied too particularly. – Nothing is so unsatisfactory in this respect as books on surgery; for instance, – what can be understood about what we call – the human heart – in the pictures of veins, fibres, and nerves that are included in those books? – Nothing. So little that one can hardly distinguish a man's heart from the heart of a rabbit. It is like the way in which houses are so badly described by those inflexible geometrical drawings that show you plans, elevations and vertical sections with such precision that one sees nothing in them. It seems to me that in these houses, as in the paintings of the man and his heart, there should be a little mingling of these two ways of explaining things: simplicity and learning, perspective and geometry.

I would like to see the footman, napkin on arm, carrying the dish of macaroni from the kitchen D, up the staircase F, to the dining-room K, while the maid is washing her lady's pots in the bedroom B. – Put the pants in the closet, the smoke in the chimney and the cat on the tiles, and set a friend to knock at the front door, and the drawing will interest people.

And the same with other things. – A little mathematics would have an excellent effect in paintings of domestic or other scenes, which have hitherto been too completely picturesque.

How amusing and instructive it would be, for example, to see, depicted with skill, a vertical section of a prudish woman offended by a naughty word!

PAUL GAVARNI TO LOUIS LEROY

London, 1848

What am I doing in London? I am dreaming, working and dreaming. Every morning I have a shot at reshaping the cosmos (I no longer concern myself with the world of politics – I settled all that long enough ago). I ask myself, for example, whether, when one comes to think of it, it would really be worth while for the inhabitants of our planet to visit the Moon, whether the journey would be worth the trouble of seeing how it can be arranged. – Pooh! it's only a trifle – but I have so little spare time. . . .

You want some 'travel impressions'; tonight, at this Drury Lane ball, something utterly fantastic happened to me. – In the first place, you must imagine one of those fine balls such as we have at the Opéra, without the hoi polloi, – a fancy-dress ball, as sumptuous as, for example, some

GAVARNI IN LONDON

EDITED BY ALBERT SMITH.

A portrait of Paul Gavarni from the title-page of 'Gavarni in London: Sketches of Life and Character', a collection of essays by various authors on different aspects of the London scene which was illustrated by the artist. Gavarni had gone to London in 1847 and the book was published two years later.

evening-dress balls before or just after 1830. – Lights, satin, diamonds and a tremendous crush – (it was not a public ball); – the orchestra occupied the back half of the stage, and behind the orchestra a suite of rooms had been kept free – rooms with gold-embroidered muslin hangings, huge mirrors and soft divans on which women sat here and there. – I strolled through, looking at everything; – coming to one of the last rooms, I walked across to a big, curtained door leading to another apartment full of more sofas and more people. I was horribly fatigued, even unwell, and dragged myself over to this last corner so as to have seen everything before going home to bed. – By chance the door was unencumbered, an open space between two crowds. – So on I went, peering through my lorgnette, and as I crossed the threshold I found myself face to face, nose to nose, with a person who was also peering through his lorgnette – and could not understand, at first, why, since the door was a wide one, this unknown fellow (in morning dress) was walking straight into me. – We looked at each other, – his was a dis-agreeable expression; the man's face was pale and sweating, he had a

'. . . tonight at this Drury Lane Ball, something utterly fantastic happened to me.' *'A Fancy-dress Ball'* – one of the artist's illustrations for *'Gavarni in London'*.

beard that I thought tousled and too long, – and there was something horrible, yet sad in the whole cast of his countenance. – I remembered! this was the dreadful face that was printed in one of the numbers of the [*Illustrated*] *London News* last January; – and then at last, waking up completely, I realized that it was *I*. – Drowsiness was leading me into a mirror, my back turned to the group of women I had been going to see. Those white *ladies* must have thought: 'What a conceited Frenchman!'

There, my good Louis, you see what work, the incessant vibration of thought, that magic cord in man which runs on two pulleys, the head and the heart, and wears them out – you see what *gin*, *stout*, and disturbing celibacy have reduced your friend to. – A thousand affectionate compliments to your gracious *mistress*.

The words in italics were written in English. A similar portrait to the one the artist mentions, with the longish beard and the rather sad expression, appeared on the title-page of 'Gavarni in London: Sketches of Life and Character'. Gavarni died in 1866.

61

THÉODORE GÉRICAULT ON THE PRIX DE ROME

Rome, 23 November 1816

It is excellent to get to know Italy, but not to remain there for as long as people make out; one well-spent year seems to me sufficient, and the five years allotted to winners of the various Prix de Rome do them more harm than good, by prolonging their studies at a time when they should rather be producing work; they thus grow accustomed to living on government money, and spend the best years of their lives in leisure and security. By the time they emerge, they have lost their vigour and become incapable of effort. And they conclude in mediocrity an existence that had at first seemed full of promise.

This is to bury the arts rather than to aid their growth, and in its initial stage the School at Rome cannot have been as it is today. Thus, many go to it, but few come back. The right and proper way to encourage all these clever young men would be by pictures to be painted for their own country, frescoes, public buildings to adorn, by laurels and pecuniary rewards – not by five years of good cooking, which fattens their bodies and destroys their souls.

I confide these observations to you alone, M——, assuring you that they are just and begging that you will not pass them on.

Théodore Géricault (1791–1824) was born at Rouen and studied under Vernet and Guérin. In 1816 he was in Rome but stayed only a year. He was impatient of Italian teaching methods, being in favour of giving up detailed preparatory drawings and painting directly on the final canvas.

THÉODORE GÉRICAULT TO HIS FRIEND M. MUSIGNY

1819

I have received your kind letter, and can have nothing more urgent or better to do than to answer it at once. Glory, seductive as you declare it to be and as I sometimes imagine it, does not yet entirely absorb me, and I devote much less care to it than that required by a true and amiable friendship. I am more flattered by your lines and your gratifying forecast of my success, than by all the articles in which insult and praise are dispensed with so much *sagacity*. Here the artist ranks with the comedian and must train himself to show complete indifference towards all that emanates from newspapers and their writers. The impassioned lover of true glory must look for it sincerely in what is beautiful and noble, and turn a deaf ear to the din raised by the pedlars of illusion.

This year our critics have reached the apex of absurdity. Every picture is judged first and foremost by the *spirit* in which it was composed. Thus, a liberal writer is to be heard praising a particular work for revealing a truly patriotic brush, a nationalist touch. The same work judged by an ultra becomes a mere revolutionary composition coloured throughout by sedition, the faces of all its figures bearing an expression of hatred for our fatherly government. A rag called the *Drapeau blanc* even accused me of slandering the entire Admiralty by the expression of one

'*The Descent from the Cross*' – *a painting after Raphael. During his stay in Italy, Géricault visited Rome and Florence and made a number of copies of the paintings of the Italian masters.*

of my faces. The poor creatures who write such imbecilities have no doubt never been through a two weeks' fast, for if they had they would know that neither poetry nor painting can convey the full horror of the situation into which the people on that raft were thrust.

There you have a sample of the glory that is to be heaped upon us here below, and of the guilty causes which may deprive us of it. Let us admit that it well deserves to be called the vanity of vanities. But I would not disdain that form of it which was dear to Pascal and which you also love.

Cordially yours,
T. Géricault

The picture referred to is the famous 'Raft of the Medusa', which was a landmark in realistic painting and shocked many of the critics. It was to have an enormous influence on the development of the Romantic movement.

'*The Raft of the Medusa*', *painted in 1819, commemorates the shipwreck of the frigate 'Medusa' three years earlier which had caused a political scandal. Géricault's masterpiece, this huge painting came as a revelation to the young Delacroix of what Romantic art should be.*

EUGÈNE DELACROIX TO J./B. PIERRET

London, 18 June 1825

. . . You do not write to me and you no doubt expect that London friends will make me forget those in Paris. You want me to break away from you and wish everything may conspire to keep me in this clime. But no: for all your forgetfulness I prefer our country, and far from seeking an affected conformity with English habits, I take pleasure in showing myself to be entirely a Frenchman. The English are not the same in their own country as in other people's, and all men are alike. They are much more obliging, much more eager to know your opinion of their country, and in return I feel a little as they are in ours: much disposed to extol France, and at their expense, which we never do in regard to them when we are at home. . . .

I saw at Wilkie's a sketch of 'Knox the Puritan preaching before Mary Stuart'. I cannot tell you how fine it is, but I fear he will spoil it; that is a fatal craze.

I have seen here a play on Faust, the most diabolical thing imaginable. The Mephistopheles is a masterpiece of caricature and intelligence. It is Goethe's *Faust*, but adapted: the principal features are preserved. They have made it into an opera mixed with comedy and with everything that is most sombre. The scene in the church is given with the priest's chanting and the organ in the distance. Impossible to carry an effect further, in the theatre. . . .

Eugène Delacroix (1798–1863), who was possibly the son of Talleyrand and who was the first French painter to come from the higher ranks of society, was the guiding spirit of the Romantic movement in French art. He was an intense admirer of Géricault, to whom many of his own characteristics (his interest in English art and in animal painting, his revolt against classical rules, his use of brilliant colour and his depiction of violent emotion) can probably be traced. This letter, written during a visit to London, gives a good idea of the kind of subjects which fired his imagination.

Already in 1824 Delacroix had been bitterly attacked by the French academic critics for his 'Massacre of Chios', a declaration of sympathy for the Greeks in their struggle for freedom, and the following letter, written on the occasion of a visit to Paris of an English theatrical company, leads us into the thick of the 'Romantic battle':

EUGÈNE DELACROIX TO VICTOR HUGO

1828

Well! A general invasion: Hamlet rears his hideous head, Othello is preparing his dagger, that essentially murderous weapon, subversive of all good theatrical government. What more, who knows ... King Lear is to tear his eyes out before a French audience. It should be a point of dignity for the Academy to declare that all imports of this kind are incompatible with public morals. Farewell good taste!

In any case, equip yourself with a stout coat of mail under your evening dress. Beware of the Classicists' daggers, or rather, sacrifice yourself valiantly for our barbarian pleasure. . . .

E.D.

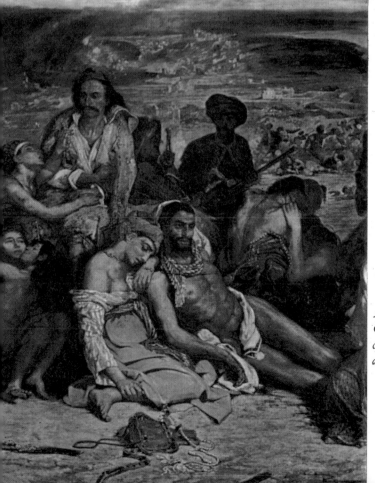

A detail from Delacroix's 'The Massacre of Chios' started in 1822 and exhibited in the Salon of 1824 when it was attacked for its brilliant colour and contemporary subject.

'The Death of Ophelia' one of a number of works by Delacroix which were inspired by the plays of Shakespeare. This painting dates from 1844.

Victor Hugo had become the leader of the Romantics with the preface to his play 'Cromwell' a year previously, and the tumultuous first night of his 'Hernani', two years later, in 1830, was to be the great victory of the school. The invasion of Paris by English players performing Shakespeare – still regarded by the classically minded, as in Voltaire's day, as the 'Barbarian' – provided a welcome opportunity to stress the new concepts and strike a blow at the Academicians. Shakespeare was a constant source of inspiration to Delacroix and he later did a series of lithographs from 'Hamlet' (see p. 76).

EUGÈNE DELACROIX TO HIS FRIEND CHARLES SOULIER

Paris, 11 March 1828

. . . I am not doing very much as yet. I am put out by this matter of the Salon. They will end by persuading me that I have produced a veritable fiasco. But I am not yet entirely convinced of it. Some say it is a complete downfall; that the 'Death of Sardanapalus' is that of the Romantics, inasmuch as Romantics do exist; others merely say that I am *inganno* [a fraud], but that they would rather be thus in error than be in the right with a thousand others who are right, perhaps, but deserving of damna﹣ tion in the name of the soul and the imagination. So I say they are all imbeciles, that the picture has its qualities and its defects, and that while there are some things I could wish to be better, there are not a few others that I think myself fortunate to have created, and which I wish them. The *Globe*, that is to say M. Vitet, says that when an imprudent soldier shoots at his friends as well as his enemies, he should be dismissed the ranks. He exhorts what he calls the young School to disown all alliance with a treacherous domination. So it seems that those who steal from me and live off my substance are disposed to denounce me louder than the rest. All this is pitiful and deserves not a moment's consideration, except insofar as its direct result is to endanger one's purely material interests, that is to say *the cash* [these two words were written in English].

You may know that my picture of 'Marino Faliero' is in the British Gallery and the English newspapers have given it splendid praise. . . .

The 'Globe' was in other respects the standard﹣bearer of the younger generation, so the artist felt doubly wounded by its attack. The Romantic movement was a rather complex affair, not the firm phalanx that it looks in retrospect. The 'Death of Sardanapalus' and 'Marino Faliero' both had subjects taken from dramas by Byron, who was, with Dante, Goethe and Shakespeare, one of Delacroix's favourite authors. He also loved music ('Colours are the music of the eye', he wrote in his 'Journal').

In 1831 the Editor of 'L'Artiste' asked Delacroix for his views on the question of competitions for artists − how to detect new talent, how to find the best and most impartial judges. 'L'Artiste' was the recently founded 'official journal' of the Romantic school:

EUGÈNE DELACROIX TO THE EDITOR OF 'L'ARTISTE'

April 1831

It was discovered that after the difficulty of persuading many people, for whom this is a new method, to enter for a competition, came the greater difficulty of finding judges, judges without passion and without pre﹣

'Some say . . . that the "Death of Sardanapalus" is that of the Romantics', *wrote Delacroix in 1827.*

judice, not liable to prefer their own friends to all others, but seeking only to do justice and promote the welfare of art. The welfare of art, Sir, is like the welfare of the country; everyone sees it in the direction to which his affections and hopes incline: justice is for everyone; the party flatters his tastes and promises him that his opinions shall triumph. Especially since the great discovery of Classicism and Romanticism, the elements of discord seem to be growing more irreconcilable. This question, which has estranged friends and divided families, does much to complicate that of competitions.

There has also been considerable perplexity as to whether the foremost aim of this method was to give employment to talent, or merely to call forth works possessing sufficient tolerable qualities to cause no scandal in the position they are to occupy. A great embarrassment for these judges, whom I assume to have been found and to be as impartial as they should. You no doubt wish me to define this second difficulty more clearly. You think that to choose talent is to give preference both to what is best and to what is most suitable; that talent triumphs over difficulties and finds no

69

'. . . my picture of "Marino Faliero" is in the British Gallery and the English newspapers have given it splendid praise.' *The subject of Delacroix's painting 'The Execution of the Doge Marino Faliero' was taken from a tragedy by Byron.*

trouble in submitting to them; alas, no, Sir, it does not submit. It loves difficulties, but only those of its own choice. It is like a thoroughbred race-horse, which will not permit all and sundry to mount it, but refuses the contest unless ridden by the master it loves. Not that talent allows itself to be carried along according to its whim, without choice and without measure; not that it rejects the yoke of reason; suitability and reason are, in brief, the essence of all it produces when genuinely inspired; but it needs that inspiration, and does not accept responsibility for what escapes it when inspiration is lacking. . . .

70

I have just had an absurd idea. I imagine the great Rubens stretched on the iron bed of a competition. I imagine him shrinking into the framework of a programme that stifles him, curtailing his gigantic forms, his beautiful exaggerations, his whole luxuriant manner. . . .

When Leo X wanted to have his palace painted, he did not go and ask his Minister of the Interior to find him whoever was worthiest; he simply chose Raphael, because he liked his talent; or perhaps only because he liked his person. You may be sure that he did not undertake the melancholy task of seeing for himself, in the efforts of thirty or forty tortured competitors, how much extravagance and absurdity can come of one poor idea when it is hounded in all directions by frenzied imaginations. The advantage to him was, no doubt, that he did not take an aversion to the subject of his fantasy even before seeing it come to birth, nor kill, in advance, the pleasure to be had from a work, by robbing it of all freshness and novelty through this strange contest, as happens to us in our competitions; for after fate or caprice has decided which artist is to get the better of the others, one feels tempted to dispense him from what he may still have to say on a worn-out theme that has lost its charm.

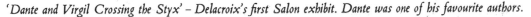

'Dante and Virgil Crossing the Styx' – Delacroix's first Salon exhibit. Dante was one of his favourite authors.

This letter is a confession of faith by Delacroix: he believed that the artist should be at liberty to follow his own inspiration instead of being shackled by academic rules or the theories of any school or movement. But if he rejected the academies he by no means rejected the great masters of the past – he greatly admired Rubens for example – and his attitude is brought out in a letter written some years later:

EUGÈNE DELACROIX TO LÉON PEISSE

15 July 1849

I ought perhaps not to say how very sound you are in everything you write, for it is I who am reaping the benefit. What you say about colour and colourists has not often been said. Criticism, like so many other things, keeps to what has been said before and does not get out of the rut. This business of the 'Beautiful', some see it in curved lines, some in straight lines, but all persist in seeing it as a matter of lines. I am now looking out of my window and I can see the most lovely countryside; lines just do not come into my head: the lark is singing, the river sparkles with a thousand diamonds, the leaves are whispering; where, I should like to know, are the lines that produce delicious impressions like these?

They refuse to see proportion or harmony except between two lines: all else they regard as chaos, and the dividers alone are judge.

Please forgive the heat of my criticism of our critics. You must understand that I humbly place myself in the shade of the great names that you cite, while giving them even higher regard than they usually receive. Oh yes, Rubens could draw. Oh yes, Correggio could draw. Not one of those men had fallen out with the Ideal. Without an Ideal there can be no painting, no drawing, no colour. And what is even worse than lacking it is to have the sham ideal they are teaching in the schools, which is enough to make the great models detested.

As I could write several volumes on this, I will stop in order to repeat how much pleasure you have given me . . .

Eug. Delacroix

Delacroix, like Rubens, was a prolific letter-writer. He also published a great deal – studies of Poussin and Prudhon, explanations of his own works, manifestoes distributed among his friends. His letters were collected at an early date, and his 'Journal', kept from 1822 to 1824 and again from 1847 to 1863, shows the great range of his interests. Meting out praise and blame to even the greatest artists, his writings are as lively and colourful as the best of his sketches.

EUGÈNE DELACROIX TO MADAME DE FORGET

Dieppe, 13 September 1852

Dear friend,

I have to remain here a little longer than I wished. So I am sending some items of sea-side news to divert you. I should have come back sooner but for the persistant bad weather, which was almost incessant for the first few days. Also, promises of one of the year's highest tides have been dangled before me for tomorrow, Tuesday. I made no resistance, particularly as, from force of habit, I have taken an enormous liking for this idle existence, although during the first few days I was almost put to flight by boredom! You do not like Dieppe, so my praise of this present visit will doubtless appear to you to be prompted by my need for rest, which had become imperative. For my part, I find the life here sufficiently varied; one has the choice between company and solitude, though it must be admitted that the latter advantage is the rarer of the two. A good deal of the boredom I felt on the first day came from my fear of meeting boring people; so I was bored by the fear of boredom. In fact it has given me a little lesson, more effective than it might appear. I have discovered that a man who wishes to extract all possible enjoyment from life must neither be constantly among diversions, nor constantly alone. The two states must mingle and alternate, the result being a desire for whichever of them is not available at the moment. One should always be desiring or hoping for something. When one can hope for that which one desires, one enjoys the greatest happiness of which our thinking apparatus is capable. To obtain what one has been desiring is the first step on the path that leads down to anxiety and uneasiness and thence to the depths of sadness and even pain, from which one can never emerge.

The sea still enchants me; I linger for three or four hours at a time on the jetty or at the edge of the cliffs. Impossible to tear oneself away. If

I could lead such a life for a certain time, coupling it with some interesting occupation, I should enjoy excellent health. For several days now I have been taking breakfast: I am less voluble in inveighing against my own epoch and against the human race: I wake up feeling pretty cheerful – a great symptom – and not at all alarmed by the approach of another day to be dragged through: in fact I find myself quite ready to be like other people. To be like other people is the real condition of happiness! Sea air and diversions are producing this miraculous effect upon me.

What you need is just the contrary. You are dying of boredom from what most mortals regard as bliss – having nothing to do. You need the treatment opposite to mine; I am not joking in the very least: one has to be compelled to some task, driven to it: anyone who is not a drunken brute must achieve boredom at all costs unless he can discover the secret of a taste for amusements.

Goodbye, dear friend. These reflections, which perhaps describe the situation that awaited you at Compiègne, are not likely to comfort you, but they will change your frame of mind for a few minutes. I shall probably be back in Paris on Thursday. Meanwhile, I send you my deepest affection.

Eug. D.

In 1857, after years of conservative opposition, Delacroix was at long last elected to the Institute, the stronghold of classicism. But he remained true to his original ideas, and was still subject to prejudice and dislike.

EUGÈNE DELACROIX TO CHARLES BAUDELAIRE

27 June 1859

Dear Sir,
How can I thank you worthily for this new evidence of your friendship? You come to my help at the moment when I am being rated by quite a number of serious critics, or who consider themselves such. These gentlemen will have only large works, and I simply sent what I had just finished, without taking a yardstick to make sure I was within the

lengths prescribed for going down to posterity, whither, I make no doubt, these gentlemen would have helped me to arrive. Having had the good fortune to please you, I can console myself for their scolding. You treat me as one only treats the *illustrious dead*; you make me blush, while giving me great pleasure; such is our nature.

Farewell, dear Sir; and I beg you, publish more often: you put something of yourself into all you do, and the admirers of your talents complain only that you appear so seldom.

With a warm handshake,

Eug. Delacroix

The Salon of 1859, where Delacroix exhibited his sketches for the frescoes he had been invited to paint in the church of Saint-Sulpice, was the most painful defeat of his always rather stormy life; even his old supporters in the Romantic movement deserted him on this occasion. In fact even Baudelaire had by no means over-praised him and the poet's true appreciation of his greatness appeared only in his obituary essay, where he compares him to the greatest masters, saying that 'Flanders has its Rubens, Italy Raphael and Veronese, France has Lebrun, David and Delacroix'.

In 1862, the year before his death, we find Delacroix remembering the performance of Faust mentioned in his letter from London thirty-seven years before:

'Jacob Wrestling with the Angel' – one of the sketches for the frescoes for St Sulpice which Delacroix exhibited in the Salon of 1859.

EUGÈNE DELACROIX TO PHILIPPE BURTY

1 March 1862

. . . I did not come to know Part II of *Faust* until long after I made my illustrations, and even then only very superficially. It struck me as an ill-digested work, of little interest from the literary standpoint, but among those most calculated to inspire a painter owing to the mixture of characters and styles it contains. If the work had been more popular, I should perhaps have taken it on. You ask what gave me the first idea of the Faust lithographs. I remember that about 1821 I saw the designs made by Retch [*sic*, i.e. Retzsch] and found them rather striking; but it was above all the performance of a dramatic opera on Faust that I saw in London in 1825 which stirred me to do something on the subject. The actor – named Terry – who is still remembered in the English theatre and who even came to Paris where, among other roles, he played King Lear, was a perfect Mephistopheles; he was fat, but that in no way diminished his nimbleness and his Satanic character.

As you know, Motte was the publisher: he had the unfortunate idea of publishing the lithographs with a text that was most damaging to their sale, quite apart from the strangeness of the plates themselves, which were caricatured on several occasions and displayed me more and more as a leading figure in the 'school of ugliness'. Still, Gérard, although he belonged to the Academy, complimented me on a few of the designs, particularly that of the tavern. I do not remember what I made out of it: something like a hundred francs, plus an engraving after Lawrence, the 'Portrait of Pius VII'. All my speculations were of that nature. The 'Hamlet' even more so: I had it printed at my own expense and published it myself. The whole thing cost me 5 or 600 francs and I did not get back half of my expenses . . .

The 'Faust lithographs' are a series of eighteen with subjects taken from Part I of Goethe's 'Faust'. They were published in Paris in 1828 with a text by Albert Stapfer. Goethe was highly pleased with them. 'The French', he said, 'reprove Delacroix for his wildness, but here it does him good service.'

The 'Hamlet' lithographs, a series of thirteen, came out in 1843 in a very small edition. Only five copies were sold at the time.

HONORÉ DAUMIER FROM PRISON TO HIS FRIEND THE
PAINTER PHILIPPE-AUGUSTE JEANRON

Sainte-Pélagie Prison, Paris
8 October 1832

My dear Genron [*sic*],
I am obliged to write to you, for I cannot come to see you, being
detained at Sainte-Pélagie by a slight indisposition. I hear a lot of noise;
I will break off my letter for a moment, you can go for a stroll in the
meantime.

Here I am, back again, it was nothing, it was only some Carlists
fighting, for those fellows are always fighting lately, not for the sake of
honour, but for domestic squabbles, or about money.

Well, here I am at Pélagie, a charming place though not everyone
enjoys it. I enjoy it, however, if only to be contrary. I assure you I

'Well, here I am at
Pélagie, a charming
place though not
everyone enjoys it.'
'*Souvenir de Ste Pélagie*'
– an early lithograph by
Daumier commemorating
his six months' stay in
the debtors' prison of
Ste Pélagie on account
of a cartoon of Louis-
Philippe. The seated
figure is reading a
Republican newspaper.

could get along pretty well in Gisquet's boarding-house, if it were not that the thought of my own home, that is to say of my family, comes to mind now and again and mars the pleasure of this agreeable solitude!!!!!!! Apart from that, prison will leave me no unpleasant memories, on the contrary; if at this moment I had a little more ink, for my ink-pot is getting empty, which is very awkward and obliges me to dip my pen every second, and that bothers me; except for that, as I say, I should not perceive myself to lack anything. I get through four times more work now I am boarded out than I did in my Papa's house. I am overwhelmed and bullied by a crowd of citizens who insist on my doing their portraits.

I am mortified, distressed, grieved, even vexed by all the reasons that prevent you from coming to see your friend the Blackguard, alias, Gargantua. I must be born to nicknames, for as soon as I arrived here, where people remembered my caricature better than my name, that of Gargantua stuck to me; but anyhow you will not believe that I have been writing to you for twenty-four hours, that is to say that at this very moment I am resuming my letter, which I set aside yesterday, interrupted by visitors and afterwards by going to dine with Geoffroy, a dinner whose sequel will be memorable in the Blackguard's annals. M. Philipon asked me if I knew of a patriotic landscape-painter, I spoke to him of Cabat and of Huet; if Cabat is not yet back, please let me know at once, because he has something he wants done in a great hurry (I mean Philipon). Don't forget to give the address of one or the other, so that they can be written to.

I am still waiting for Landon, who was to come and see me; he need only arm himself with his diploma, and all the other papers that prove his identity, in order to get into Pélagie with no difficulty. It would give me the greatest pleasure; try to see him and persuade him to come.

I shall await your reply with impatience. Answer at once about Cabat and Huet.

My respects to your family.

Farewell the Blackguard.   H.D.

He is still amid these charms. Do not mention politics, because letters are opened.

Honoré Daumier (1808–1879) had been sentenced to six months in the prison of Sainte-Pélagie on account of his lithograph 'Gargantua', which showed King Louis-Philippe in the guise of the famous Rabelaisian character being fed with gold coins by his senators and ministers and defecating orders, portfolios and marshals' batons. Not unnaturally, this was regarded by the authorities as going too far. Gisquet was the Prefect of the Paris Police. Jeanron, to whom the letter was written, became director of the national art museums after the 1848 revolution, and founded the Musée du Luxembourg. Philipon was the editor of 'La Caricature'; Cabat and Huet were friends and fellow-painters.

Daumier earned his living, reluctantly, as a pictorial journalist, and cartoonist, producing some 4,000 lithographs for 'La Caricature', 'Le Charivari' and similar journals. He always longed to paint seriously but it was not until the last years of his life that his friends, including Corot, managed to persuade the art-dealer Durand-Ruel to hold an exhibition.

'La République.' This oil sketch was Daumier's first important serious painting and dates from 1848. It was painted for a competition for a picture symbolizing the new Republic which was to replace the official portrait of Louis-Philippe who had just been deposed in the Revolution of the same year.

Corot sketching at Ville-d'Avray', a wash drawing by Honoré Daumier.

CAMILLE COROT DESCRIBES THE BEGINNING OF A LAND-SCAPE PAINTER'S DAY

Gruyères, 1857

You know, a landscape painter's day is delightful. You get up early, at three o'clock in the morning, before sunrise; you go and sit under a tree; you watch and wait. At first there is nothing much to be seen. Nature looks like a whitish canvas with a few broad outlines faintly sketched in; all is misty, everything quivers in the cool dawn breeze. The sky lights up. The sun has not yet burst through the gauze veil that hides the meadow, the little valley, the hills on the horizon. The nocturnal vapours are still creeping in silvery flakes over the frozen green of the grass. Ah! a first ray of sunshine! The tiny flowers seem to wake up happily. Each has its tremulous dewdrop. The leaves shiver with cold in the morning breeze. Invisible birds are singing beneath the leaves. It seems as though the flowers were saying their prayers. Little butterfly-winged cupids frolic over the meadow, making the tall grass ripple. One sees nothing. Everything is there! The whole landscape lies behind the transparent gauze of the fog that now rises, drawn upwards by the sun, and, as it rises, reveals the silver-spangled river, the fields, the trees, the cottages, the further scene. At last one can discern all that one could only guess at before.

The sun is up! There is a peasant at the end of the field, with his waggon drawn by a yoke of oxen. You can hear the little bell round the neck of the ram, the leader of the flock. Everything is bursting into life, sparkling in the full light – light which as yet is still soft and golden. The background, simple in line and harmonious in colour, melts into the infinite expanse of sky, through the bluish, misty atmosphere. The flowers raise their heads, the birds flutter hither and thither. A country-man on a white horse rides away down the steep-banked lane. The little rounded willows on the bank of the stream look like birds spreading their tails. It's adorable! and one paints! and paints! . . .

'Une Matinée. La danse des nymphes' by Corot. Not even the Impressionists could surpass Corot in portraying nature at her most delicate – 'the silver-spangled river . . . the bluish, misty atmosphere . . . the background, melting into the infinite expanse of the sky'.

This little piece was jotted down while Corot was staying in Switzerland with his friend Daniel Bovy at the Château de Gruyères in 1857. Corot was sixty years old. Beginning as a traditional classical painter, he had evolved by the 1850's a purely personal landscape style, poetic but at the same time based on close observation of nature. Simple and generous by nature, he painted for the sheer joy of it. Another jotting reads:

CAMILLE COROT'S NOTES IN AN ALBUM

Châtelaine

Be guided solely by feeling. Only, being mere mortals, we are prone to error; listen to comments; but follow only those you understand, and which must fuse with your own feeling. – Firmness: docility. – Follow your convictions. It is better to be nothing than to be the echo of other painters. As the sage observed, when one follows anybody, one is always behind. Beauty in art is truth steeped in the impression made upon us by the sight of nature. I am struck on seeing some place or other. While seeking conscious imitation, I do not for an instant lose the emotion that first gripped me. Reality forms part of art; feeling completes it. In nature, seek first of all for form; then for the values or relationship between tints, for colour and style; and the whole must obey the feeling you have had. Whatever we feel is perfectly real. A particular view, or object, moves us by a certain elegant grace. We must never depart from that, and in seeking for truth and accuracy we must never forget to give it that cloak that impressed us. Whatever the view, or the object, we must surrender to the first impression. If we have been really touched, the sincerity of our feeling will be conveyed to other people. . . .

Corot died in 1875. A few days before he died he is recorded to have said this to one of his friends:

CAMILLE COROT TO HIS FRIEND M. FRANÇAIS

1875

If my time has come I shall have nothing to complain of. For fifty-three years I have been painting; so I have been able to devote myself entirely to what I loved best in the world; I have never suffered poverty; I had good parents and excellent friends; I can only thank God.

ADOLF VON MENZEL TO HIS FRIEND AND PATRON HEINRICH
ARNOLD

Berlin, 29 December 1836

First of all, my warmest thanks for Dürer's 'St Hubert', a present which
has given me quite exceptional pleasure; it now remains to achieve in
our own period what that Phoenix achieved in his. We shall probably
not bring it off, I believe that the entire present generation of artists (I
mean those who are now our greatest, the standard-bearers; I do not
refer to the motley crew running behind the banner, for the day will
come when their pictures and even their graves will be forgotten) is only
the forerunner of the age which will be able to manage that, we have
enough to do to bite our way through the old leaven; it is for us to do
the climbing, it will be left for our successors to reach the top. Many
people consider that 'John Huss', 'Jeremiah' and the 'Sons of Edward'
represent the supreme achievement of present-day art, I would prefer to
think of them as a step towards it. From the earliest ages, the arts have
only created and achieved what was wanted at a given time; when faith
was the living principle of the human mind it was also that of art
(whether in classical times or in the Middle Ages). When a spiritual
trend in a particular country or nation has reached its culminating point,
it sinks down, through every possible labyrinth and abyss, until a new
trend is recognized in it. Thus, the Reformation was the culminating
point of faith, and it followed the course I have just described until now,
when people are beginning to become aware that understanding is the

'The Lion in Love' by Roqueplan and 'The Storm' by Gudin – two of the French artists admired by Menzel.

principle at which they are aiming. Art has gone hand in hand with intellectual development all through its progress and its deviations, and will always do so, because artists, like the rest of mankind, have their share in that development and in the demands made upon it. So in my opinion the propensity of our art to move in that direction is not a devia-tion, but the logical outcome of a reviving spirit of the age; and I think that what still disturbs us and leaves us unsatisfied is its incompleteness; it is still clinging to the immediate past, though many people do not yet realize this.

Even if art ultimately takes a decided turn in this direction, there is no need for it to develop into an arithmetical problem . . . In due course we shall have men with minds wherein the age will work decisively enough for them to set about things in the right way. The really brilliant, high-principled materialism of the present-day French artists (those who represent the school and have helped to create it) – men like Gudin, Roqueplan, Coignet, Watelet up to a point, and Le Poittevin – will bring about a revolution in this respect, in which those in that country who believe that to paint in bright colours is brilliant and that glibness is witty, will meet their downfall, which can do no harm, while those who are strong enough to survive will certainly be the better for it. The French (in general) are perhaps one-sided in aesthetic matters, but we are the same in a certain sense (only in the other extreme), and I and many others hope that the impression we absorb from their work will jerk us out of our one-sided attitude. We ought not to turn into French artists and we do not want to; but we should respectfully recognize that there is much good in them, and learn from it.

Adolf von Menzel (1815–1905) was a highly successful German 'history painter'. He spent nearly all his life in Berlin, where most of his works now are, large patriotic compositions, remarkable for historical accuracy and charm of colour. But he also produced some vigorous studies of contemporary life, the beginning of the industrial period (such as his 'Iron Rolling-mill'), and views of Berlin. Gudin, Roqueplan, Coignet, Watelet and Le Poittevin were famous artists in their day with a fondness for Romantic subjects, but their reputation has failed to live up to Menzel's prediction.

ARNOLD BÖCKLIN TO COLONEL MERIAN-ISELIN

Rome, 26 September 1865

Dear Sir,

All this summer I have been prevented by various reasons from answering your kind letter. To begin with I had a fever for several weeks, which left me weak and with no courage to work – and recovered only when the great heat was beginning. All this had its effect on the picture too, and what with the heat and the doubts that combined to torment me, several months went by before I could again see a smooth road ahead. As everyone knows who is not made of stone, a situation like this does not make one communicative, and I therefore feel sure I can rely on your indulgence. Because I was dissatisfied with the work, I postponed taking the photographs too, wanting to spare you a depressing sight by waiting till the picture was more advanced.

Your remark that an easel picture should not be treated like a decoration, but carried out as the expression of a definite practical mood, precisely reflects my view concerning this picture. In others, detail may perhaps predominate, in yet others the decorative aspect; in each case this depends on the leading, basic ideas, which are conditioned by the outlook of the individual artist – it would take too long to discuss that here. My own view is that a picture should not weary the beholder – that while each particular feature should be in tune with the whole, and sometimes in quite a subordinate way, it should be beautiful in itself. The fine arts are not intended for man's torment, but for his enjoyment. To achieve this practical skill I have made all kinds of technical experiments in the last few years, but I have not ventured to make use of them in your picture, because I have reliable evidence of the lasting qualities of oil painting which, when suitably handled, is capable of a perfection and a beauty of colour seldom credited to this medium. I now think I shall be finished by December or January, but I would like to wait another few weeks so as to hear opinions and be able to make any necessary corrections. Up to now I have kept the work carefully hidden, in order not to be led astray by premature comments. At a later stage, however, an expert opinion becomes indispensable, because the eye can grow accustomed even to mistakes, and I will even venture to ask you yourself for your opinion. I can have no objection to a little extra work when it gives me the opportunity to complete the picture to your satisfaction and my own.

Meantime I shall most gratefully avail myself of your kind offer to send me a further advance, and should be much obliged if you would send it within the month.

With great respect,
Your devoted
A. Böcklin

Arnold Böcklin (1827–1901) was a Swiss painter who spent much of his life in Italy and died at Fiesole. In his early period he painted delicate, charming landscapes, which he sometimes populated with fabulous beings in the classical style, giving them a poetic atmosphere or turning them into mythological scenes. For a long time he had a hard struggle, but his strange, imaginative pictures were a stimulus to contemporary poets and writers, and largely thanks to them he was praised as a great artist at the close of his life. After his death the critics and painters resumed their attacks, but he has now found his niche in the history of nineteenth-century art.

'The fine arts are . . . for man's enjoyment.' *'Shepherd Boy with Flute' – a typical work by Böcklin.*

'I cannot conceal from you that I am often smitten with the deepest sadness.' *A self-portrait by Hans von Marées.*

HANS VON MARÉES TO K. FIEDLER (?)

Rome, 1867

It is a long while since you last heard from me; but much as my heart needs to pour itself out to you, I have been in such a melancholy mood all this time, my whole being tossed hither and thither by doubts, that I wished to spare you the melancholy sight of an existence thus fraught with strife. Like Ahasuerus I was roaming to and fro with no rest or peace – in the spiritual if not in the bodily sense. A thousand times I said to myself, 'Be a man, set to work and concentrate on your work.' But that is easier said than done. 'If you exert your will', people would say to me, 'you can move mountains.' Who would not wish to do that? He who knows his own will is half way to his goal. But to will without knowing what: there you have the confession, wrested at last from my distraught soul. You are right to scold me for my lack of trust, to which you have a more than justified claim. I cannot conceal from you that I am often smitten with the deepest sadness when I look back and think how lively, bold and frank I was in my early days. I thought nature had intended me to be a battering-ram and that honesty and sound judgment would guide me towards the truth. Time rushes on, as it always has done; but people nowadays are trying to outstrip time. They tear onward, from today into tomorrow, in a way the world has never seen before. And I, poor limping fellow, cannot keep pace with them; for a long time I have made no progress, if anything I have even fallen back.

But why all this terrible haste, where the devil are they all making for? I don't know. It seems to me that in the end people will realize that with all their haste they have cut themselves down to a tenth of their allotted span. Aha – now I am beginning to see what I want; I want to live, I want to look upon life as a gift from God (which indeed it is), I want to prize and economize it, to use it as an inexhaustible source of activity, so that every passing minute may reveal some unknown aspect of this precious gift. The only question is, how to begin. I am no prophet, I cannot predict what will happen, or say how the unknown will influence my behaviour. But I can make up my mind what I do not intend to do; the past, with its experience, will help me there. Allow me that much, gentlemen, so that, purified and liberated, I may devote myself to your service.

Another day has gone by, no idle one it is true, yet it has shown once again the vanity of human purposes. Just as our earth turns daily towards the light and then away from it, so man moves in a perpetual orbit from good to evil. Will he never succeed in beholding the light in its unchanging radiance? Does day exist only in order to make way for night?

Hans von Marées (1837–1887) studied in Berlin and worked for eight years in Munich, but he spent most of his later life in Italy. It is not quite certain to whom this letter, which exists in draft only, was addressed, but it shows Marées in a mood of discouragement and despondency, and, indeed, at the end of his life he ceased to exhibit his work completely. His frescoes for the Naples Zoological Museum are among the most powerful works of German nineteenth-century painting.

WILHELM LEIBL TO HIS MOTHER

Berbling, 18 March 1879

Here, in the open country and among those who live close to nature, one can paint naturally. My stay in Munich served to confirm my belief that painting, in that town, is simply a habit, carried on with a shrewd eye to expediency, but quite without original feeling or any independent outlook. Whether it be called historical painting, genre or landscape, that kind of thing is not art; it is merely a superficial copying of things familiar to the point of satiety.

Wilhelm Leibl (1844–1900) had studied at Munich and his early works were painted in a free and broad style, which won acclaim in Paris, where he went for a year and came under the influence of Courbet. But he later changed his style and adopted a manner of meticulous realism. The picture on which he was working at

Ludwig I, shown surrounded by artists and scholars in this picture by Wilhelm von Kaulbach, had made Munich one of the art-centres of Europe earlier in the century. Leibl in 1879 was not impressed.

the time of this letter was 'Three Peasant Women in a Village Church', now in the Kunsthalle of Hamburg. It took nearly four years to paint. It is doubtful whether any painter since medieval times has ever spent so much time and trouble over a single canvas. Its progress is told in further letters over the years:

WILHELM LEIBL TO HIS MOTHER

Berbling, 20 May 1879

It really takes great staying-power to bring such a difficult, detailed picture to completion in the circumstances. Most of the time I have literally taken my life in my hands in order to paint it. For up to now the church has been as cold as the grave, so that one's fingers get completely stiff. Sometimes, too, it is so dark that I have the greatest difficulty in getting a clear enough view of the part on which I am working. I need hardly say that work like this can be completely upset by even the faintest idea of finishing it by a particular date. So you must begin to accustom yourself to the thought that you will not find me represented at the Munich exhibition. But do not feel uneasy. Even if the picture is not exhibited, it will have its effect. Several peasants came to look at it just lately, and they instinctively folded their hands in front of it. One man said, 'That is the work of a master.' I have always set greater store by the opinion of simple peasants than by that of so-called painters, so I take that peasant's remark as a good omen.

November 1879

You are mistaken in assuming that the picture is nearly finished by now. If you could only see it, you would cease once and for all to imagine that such a thing could be painted in the time you suppose. I always have to pay dearly when I try to go quickly, because the sight of the hurriedly painted portions annoys me so much that I cannot leave them as they are, I have to clean them off completely and begin all over again.

26 June 1880

I am still working in the sweat of my brow, simply so as to inch forward a little every day. It is really enough to drive one out of one's mind, and requires cast-iron patience.

15 November 1880

I cannot complain of my health, on the contrary I feel perfectly well, though I am still working in the church every day. But I have been having very bad luck with the picture. For instance, I could not finish the hands of the last figure, because when I had already got a long way with them the model developed a boil – and an inflammation of the eye, so that I could not finish the head either. My patience is being sorely tried.

Leibl finished the picture at last in the summer of 1881.

'Three Peasant Women in a Village Church' by Wilhelm Leibl. The story of this painting, which took him four years to complete, is told in his letters. Much of the work was done on the spot, in a church 'as cold as the grave, so that one's fingers get completely stiff'.

DANTE GABRIEL ROSSETTI TO WILLIAM ALLINGHAM

London, January 1861

We have got our rooms quite jolly now. Our drawing-room is a beauty, I assure you, already, and on the first country trip we make we shall have it newly papered from a design of mine which I have an opportunity of getting made by a paper manufacturer, somewhat as below. I shall have it printed on common brown packing-paper and on blue grocer's-paper, to try which is best.

The trees are to stand the whole height of the room, so that the effect will be slighter and quieter than in the sketch where the tops look too large. Of course they will be wholly conventional: the stems and fruit will be Venetian red, the leaves black – the fruit, however, will have a line of yellow to indicate roundness and distinguish it from the stem; the lines of the ground black, and the stars yellow with a white ring round them. The red and black will be made of the same key as the brown or blue of the ground, so that the effect of the whole will be rather sombre, but I think rich, also. When we get the paper up, we shall have the doors and wainscoting painted summer-house green. We got into the room in such a hurry that we had no time to do anything to

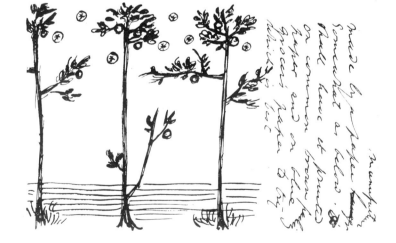

'The trees are to stand the whole height of the room' – *Rossetti's letter of January 1861 contains this sketch for the wall-paper he was proposing for his drawing-room.*

*'Beata Beatrix.' Rossetti
has here portrayed his wife,
Elizabeth Siddal, as
Dante's Beatrice in Paradise.
This drawing is a study for
the painting now in the
National Gallery, London.*

the paper and painting, which had just been done by the landlord. I
should like you to see how nice the rooms are looking, and how many
nice things we have got in them.

However you have yet to see a real wonder of the age – viz., Topsy's
house, which baffles all description now.

We are organising (but this is quite under the rose as yet) a company
for the production of furniture and decoration of all kinds, for the sale of
which we are going to open an actual shop! The men concerned are
Madox Brown, Jones, Topsy, Webb (the architect of T.'s House), P. P.
Marshall, Faulkner, and myself. Each of us is now producing, at his own

Rossetti's self-portrait at the age of twenty-seven, five years before his marriage.

charges, one or two (and some of us more) things towards the stock. We are not intending to compete with ——'s costly rubbish or anything of that sort, but to give real good taste at the price as far as possible of ordinary furniture. We expect to start in some shape about May or June, but not to go to any expense in premises at first.

This letter dates from the happiest period of Rossetti's life. He had married Elizabeth Siddal the year before and was busy setting up a home near Blackfriars Bridge. The 'company' was 'Morris, Marshall, Faulkner & Co.' (later to become 'Morris and Co.'), founded by William Morris ('Topsy') to provide good honest (i.e. hand-made) furniture, wall-paper, tapestries, carpets, stained glass, etc. 'Topsy's house' is the Red House, Bexleyheath, designed by Philip Webb in 1859 and containing furnishings by other members of the circle.

Rossetti's happiness did not last. His wife died the next year and he himself became a recluse and drug-addict. He is remembered chiefly as one of the founders of the Pre-Raphaelite Brotherhood (1849), which rejected post-Renaissance art and tried to return to the piety and simplicity of the Florentine Quattrocento painters. The group soon broke up, but its members continued to exercise influence. Rossetti went on to paint and write poems on subjects mostly drawn from Dante and the Middle Ages. To the mid-Victorians he was a 'picturesque figure', a Bohemian in an otherwise shrewd and practical circle. He died in 1882.

EDWARD BURNE-JONES DESCRIBES HIS FIRST MEETING
WITH ROSSETTI

I had no dream of ever knowing Rossetti, but I wanted to look at him,
and as I had heard that he taught in the Working Men's College in
Great Ormond Street, a little University set up by Denison Maurice,
where men skilled in science or history gave lectures and their services of
evenings, I went to the College one day to find out how it would be
possible that I should set eyes upon him. I was told that there was to be a
monthly meeting that very evening in a room connected with the College,
and that, for a modest payment, anyone could get admittance, including
tea, and hear the addresses on the condition of the College and the
advancement of studies which were delivered by the different professors –
so without fail I was there, and sat at a table and had thick bread and
butter, but knowing no one. But good fellowship was the rule there, that
was clear, and a man sitting opposite to me spoke at once to me, introducing himself by the name of Furnivall, and I gave my name and college
and my reason for coming. He reached across the table to a kindly-
looking man whom he introduced to me as Vernon Lushington, to
whom I repeated my reason for coming, and begged him to tell me
when Rossetti entered the room. It seemed that it was doubtful if he
would appear at all, that he was constant in his work of teaching
drawing at the College, but had no great taste for the nights of addresses
and speeches, and as I must have looked downcast at this, Lushington,
with a kindness never to be forgotten by me, invited me to go to his
rooms in Doctors Commons a few nights afterwards, where Rossetti
had promised to come. So I waited a good hour, or more, listening to
speeches about the progress of the College, and Maurice, who was
president, spoke of Macaulay's new volume, just out, blaming much the
attack on George Fox in a true Carlylese spirit, which was very pleasing
– and then Lushington whispered to me that Rossetti had come in, and
so I saw for the first time, his face satisfying all my worship, and I
listened to addresses no more, but had my fill of looking, only I would
not be introduced to him. You may be sure I sent a long letter about all
this to Morris at Walthamstow, and on the night appointed, about ten

o'clock I went to Lushington's rooms where was a company of men, some of whom have been friends ever since. I remember Saffi was there, and Rossetti's brother William, and by and bye Rossetti came, and I was taken up to him and had my first fearful talk with him. Browning's *Men and Women* had just been published a few days before, and some-one speaking disrespectfully of that book was rent in pieces at once for his pains, and was dumb for the rest of the evening – so that I saw my hero could be a tyrant and I thought it sat finely upon him. Also another unwary man professed an interest in metaphysics; he also was dealt with firmly.

Before I left that night Rossetti bade me come to his studio the next day. It was in the last house by Blackfriars Bridge at the North West corner of the bridge, long ago pulled down to make way for the Embankment; and I found him painting at a water colour of a monk copying a mouse in an illumination. The picture was called 'Fra Pace' afterwards.

He received me very courteously, and asked much about Morris, one or two of whose poems he knew already, and I think that was our principal subject of talk, for he seemed much interested about him. He shewed me many designs for pictures: they tossed about everywhere in the room; the floor at one end was covered with them, and with books. No books were on the shelves, and I remember long afterwards he once said that books were no use to a painter except to prop up models in difficult positions, and that then they might be very useful. No one seemed to be in attendance upon him. I stayed long and watched him at work, not knowing till many a day afterwards that this was a thing he greatly hated – and when for shame I could stay no longer, I went away, having carefully concealed from him the desire I had to be a painter.

Edward Burne-Jones (1833–1898) was the youngest member of the Pre-Raphaelite Brotherhood and for nearly half a century he was the most in-fluential exponent of this reform movement which tried to bring a 'new beauty' into every branch of art including furnishing and decoration.

His first meeting with Rossetti described above took place in January 1856. Burne-Jones was then twenty-three and studying at Oxford University to become a clergyman, as was his inseparable friend William Morris ('Topsy' to his friends there). Disappointed by university life they wished to leave and 'begin a life of art'. Rossetti's illustration to William Allingham's 'Elfen Mere' had come as a revelation to Burne-Jones of what drawing should be and he had come to London hoping to see his idol. On Rossetti's advice he abandoned his studies and gave himself up to art with Rossetti as his master. Through him he was soon to meet another member of the Pre-Raphaelite circle – Holman Hunt – whose painting 'The Light of the World' had also aroused his enthusiasm at Oxford:

EDWARD BURNE-JONES TO HIS FATHER
1856

A glorious day it has been – a glorious day, one to be remembered by the side of the most notable ones in my life: for whilst I was painting and Topsy was making drawings in Rossetti's studio, there entered the greatest genius that is on earth alive, William Holman Hunt – such a grand-looking fellow, such a splendour of a man, with a great wiry golden beard, and faithful violet eyes – oh, such a man. And Rossetti sat by him and played with his golden beard passing his paint-brush through the hair of it. And all evening through Rossetti talked most gloriously, such talk as I do not believe any man could talk beside him.

Morris' original ambition on leaving Oxford was to become an architect and in 1859 he embarked on his cherished scheme of building a house to his own specifications, with the help of his friend Philip Webb, at Bexleyheath in Kent. When the house was completed the following year, Burne-Jones was invited down to discuss and help with its decoration.

EDWARD BURNE-JONES' DESCRIPTION OF WILLIAM
MORRIS' HOUSE

The house was strongly built of red brick, and red tiles: the porches were deep and the plan of the house was two sides of a quadrangle. In the angle was a covered well. As we talked of decorating it plans grew apace. We fixed upon a romance for the drawing-room, a great favourite of ours called Sir Degrevaunt. I designed seven pictures from that poem, of which I painted three that summer and autumn in tempera. We schemed also subjects from Troy for the hall, and a great ship carrying Greek heroes for a larger space in the hall, but these remained only as schemes, none were designed except the ship. The great settle from Red Lion Square, with the three painted shutters above the seat, was put up at the end of the drawing-room, and there was a ladder to its top and a parapet round it, and a little door above, in the wall behind it, that led into the roof. There at Christmas time it was intended that minstrels should play and sing. I began a picture from the *Niebelungen Lied* on the inside of one of the shutters of this settle, and Morris painted in tempera a hanging below the Degrevaunt pictures, of bushy trees and parrots and labels on which he wrote the motto he adopted for his life, 'If I can'. He worked hard at this and the room began to look very beautiful.

Burne-Jones was at this time attempting to revive the art of painting in tempera directly upon the wall. 'Sir Degrevaunt' was a fifteenth-century English romance. It was to provide furnishings in good taste for this house that the firm of 'Morris and Co.' was originally formed.

'. . . there entered the greatest genius that is on earth alive, William Holman Hunt' – *one of the founders of the Pre-Raphaelite Brotherhood, his painting 'The Light of the World' had aroused the enthusiasm of the young Burne-Jones.*

A woodcut illustration by Rossetti to 'Goblin Market', one of his sister Christina's poems which appeared in 1862. His monogram and that of Morris, Marshall, Faulkner & Co. appear in the bottom corners.

"Buy from us with @ golden curl"

EDWARD BURNE-JONES TO HIS WIFE'S SISTER

1862

I am determined to labour in every direction to get good engraving again, and I shall need you beyond words – so work, my little darling, like anything.

I see that for the engraving I want, the most perfect design and beautiful drawing is needed, more than in pictures even, for in them so many other qualities come in and have their say, and a picture may be great if it has only one quality pre-eminently grand. But in engraving every faculty is needed – simplicity, the hardest of all things to learn – restraint in leaving out every idea that is not wanted (and perhaps fifty come where five are wanted) – perfect outline, as correct as can be without effort, and, still more essentially, neat – and a due amount of quaintness. I really do not think anyone in England could have engraved the Rethels. Rossetti, in despair, gave a very careful block to Faulkner the other day, and that ingenious man's first attempt is a regular triumph – it is an illustration to Miss Rossetti's poems, coming out in February, so you will see it.

'Dance of Death', one of a series of wood-engravings by the German artist, Alfred Rethel, which Burne-Jones admired for their simplicity and wished to emulate.

By absolutely perfect wood-engraving, I mean such work as all the sixteenth-century engravings and such as those quite perfect examples in Rethel's 'Dance of Death' and the 'Friend and Avenger'. I don't believe that any attempt to express more than they do could possibly be successful.

As to scribbly work, it enrages one beyond endurance. Nearly all book and periodical illustration is full of it – drawings, you know the kind, that have wild work in all the corners, stupid, senseless rot that takes an artist half a minute to sketch and an engraver half a week to engrave, for scribble is fearful labour to render. My dear, look at most things in *Once a Week* – the wasted time of poor engravers in rendering all that scrawl, if rightly used, might fill England with beautiful work.

'. . . for the engraving I want, the most perfect design and beautiful drawing is needed.' *One of the eighty-seven wood-engravings designed by Burne-Jones for an edition of 'The Works of Geoffrey Chaucer' published in 1896. This book was the masterpiece of William Morris' Kelmscott Press.*

Incipit secunda pars ❀ ❀ ❀ ❀ ❀ ❀

FER FRO THILKE PALAYS HONUR-
ABLE
Theras this markys shoop his mariage,
Ther stood a throop, of site delitable,
In which that povre folk of that village
Hadden hir beestes and hir herbergage,
And of hire labour tooke hir sustenance,
After that the erthe yaf hem habundance.

AMONGES thise povre folk ther
dwelte a man
Which that was holden povrest of
hem alle;
But hye God som tyme senden kan
His grace into a litel oxes stalle:
Janicula men of that throop hym calle.
A doghter hadde he, fair ynogh to sighte,
And Grisildis this yonge mayden highte.

But for to speke of vertuous beautee,
Thanne was she oon the faireste under sonne;
For povreliche yfostred up was she,
No likerous lust was thurgh hire herte yronne;
Wel ofter of the welle than of the tonne
She drank, and for she wolde vertu plese,
She knew wel labour, but noon ydel ese.

But thogh this mayde tendre were of age,
Yet in the brest of hire virginitee
Ther was enclosed rype and sad corage,
And in greet reverence and charitee
Hir olde povre fader fostred shee;
A fewe sheep, spynnynge, on feeld she kepte,
She wolde noght been ydel til she slepte.

And whan she homward cam, she wolde brynge
Wortes, or other herbes, tymes ofte,

Burne-Jones goes on to confess his own desire to publish '100,000 wood-cuts as big as "Death the Friend" or bigger'. The only way to engrave on wood, he says, is 'very simply, with little or no cross-hatching, and no useless clever-ness, and no attempt to do anything that copper or steel would do a thousand times better'. *The letter concludes with the following postscript:*

Keep up drawing the whole time through, say at the least half the day, and let it be from nature – faces, best of all, because hardest. Practise at anything that will reveal its mistakes most glaringly; not a foliage, because a hundred errors may be concealed in the general confusion, nor even drapery, but bare arms, necks, noses, tops of heads &c. wherein one faltering step turns everything to ridicule.

The art of book illustration and wood-engraving had sunk to a very low level in England by the middle of the nineteenth century. 'Once a Week' was a miscellany started in 1859 in which a number of young artists, who had joined together with the object of raising the standard, published their work. Burne-Jones' book illustrations are not very numerous. The majority were done for Morris – the most important being for his elaborately designed edition of the works of Chaucer published at the Kelmscott Press. Like Rossetti and Morris, Burne-Jones did not limit himself to one field and in addition he also executed designs for stained glass, mosaics, tapestries and needlework.

Burne-Jones enjoyed an enormous success with the public and some of his statements on art are well expressed and of interest as they represent a certain view of art current at the end of the nineteenth century.

EDWARD BURNE-JONES ON THE ART OF PORTRAITURE

Of course my faces have no expression in the sense in which people use the word. How should they have any? They are not portraits of people in paroxysms – paroxysms of terror, hatred, benevolence, desire, avarice, veneration, and all the 'passions' and 'emotions' that Le Brun and that kind of person find so *magnifique* in Raphael's later work – mostly painted by his pupils and assistants by the way. It is Winckelmann, isn't it, who says that when you come to the age of expression in Greek art you have come to the age of decadence? I don't remember how or where it is said, but of course it is true – can't be otherwise in the nature of things.

Portraiture may be great art. There is a sense, indeed, in which it is perhaps the greatest art of any. And portraiture involves expression. Quite true, but expression of what? Of a passion, an emotion, a mood? Certainly not. Paint a man or woman with the damned 'pleasing expression' or even the 'charmingly spontaneous' so dear to the 'photo-graphic artist', and you see at once that the thing is a mask, as silly as the old tragic and comic mask. The only expression allowable in great portraiture is the expression of character and moral quality, not of anything temporary, fleeting, accidental. Apart from portraiture you don't want even so much, or very seldom: in fact you only want types, symbols, suggestions. The moment you give what people call expression, you destroy the typical character of heads and degrade them into portraits which stand for nothing.

EDWARD BURNE-JONES ON REALISM IN ART

1895

One of the hardest things in the world is to determine how much realism is allowable in any particular picture. It is of so many different kinds, too. For instance, I want a shield or a crown or a pair of wings or what not, to look real. Well, I make what I want, or a model of it,

A study by Burne-Jones for 'Lancelot's Vision of the Grail'. The Arthurian romances were a frequent source of inspiration to the Pre-Raphaelites.

and then make studies from that. So that what eventually gets on to the canvas is a reflection of a reflection of something purely imaginary. The three Magi never had crowns like that, supposing them to have had crowns at all, but the effect is realistic because the crown from which the studies were made is real – and so on.

Realism? Direct transcript from Nature? I suppose by the time the 'photographic artist' can give us all the colours as correctly as the shapes, people will begin to find out that the realism they talk about isn't art at all but science; interesting, no doubt, as a scientific achievement, but nothing more. Someone will have succeeded in making a reflection in a looking-glass permanent under certain conditions. What has that to do with art?

Burne-Jones was made a baronet in 1894 and died in 1898.

An earthenware tile panel with nine scenes from the story of Sleeping Beauty designed by Burne-Jones surrounded by swan tiles by Philip Webb.

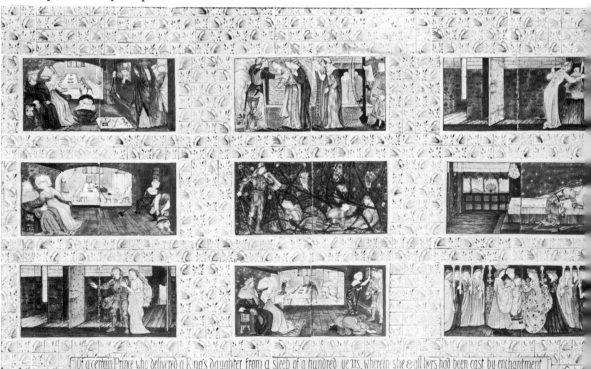

William Morris

WILLIAM MORRIS TO THE 'MANCHESTER EXAMINER'

March, 1883

It was the purpose of my lecture to raise another question than one of mere art. I specially wished to point out that the question of popular art was a social question, involving the happiness or misery of the greater part of the community. The absence of popular art from modern times is more disquieting and grievous to bear for this reason than for any other, that it betokens that fatal division of men into the cultivated and the degraded classes which competitive commerce has bred and fosters; popular art has no chance of a healthy life, or, indeed, of a life at all, till we are on the way to fill up this terrible gulf between riches and poverty. Doubtless many things will go to filling it up, and if art must be one of those things, let it go. What business have we with art at all unless all can share it? I am not afraid but that art will rise from the dead,

'Music', one of four stained-glass panels designed by Dante Gabriel Rossetti and executed by Morris, Marshall, Faulkner & Co.

A scene from the legend of St George. This drawing was made by Morris for a cabinet designed by Philip Webb. It was the aim of Morris, Marshall, Faulkner & Co. to bring beauty and craftsmanship into objects of everyday use.

whatever else lies there. For, after all, what is the true end and aim of all politics and all commerce? Is it not to bring about a state of things in which all men may live at peace and free from over-burdensome anxiety, provided with work which is pleasant to them and produces results useful to their neighbours?

It may well be a burden to the conscience of an honest man who lives a more manlike life to think of the innumerable lives which are spent in toil unrelieved by hope and uncheered by praise; men who might as well, for all the good they are doing to their neighbours by their work,

The William Morris room at the Victoria and Albert Museum, London.

be turning a crank with nothing at the end of it; but this is the fate of those who are working at the bidding of blind competitive commerce, which still persists in looking at itself as an end, and not as a means.

It has been this burden on my conscience, I do in all sincerity believe, which has urged me on to speak of popular art in Manchester and elsewhere. I could never forget that in spite of all drawbacks my work is little else than pleasure to me; that under no conceivable circumstances would I give it up even if I could. Over and over again have I asked myself why should not my lot be the common lot. My work is simple work enough; much of it, nor that the least pleasant, any man of decent intelligence could do, if he could but get to care about the work and its results. Indeed I have been ashamed when I have thought of the contrast between my happy working hours and the unpraised, unrewarded, monotonous drudgery which most men are condemned to. Nothing shall convince me that such labour as this is good or necessary to civilization.

William Morris (1834–1896) was painter, textile-designer, typographer, publisher, poet and social reformer. This letter, which follows a lecture he gave to the Manchester Royal Institution in March 1883 in which he advocated Socialist doctrines in connection with art, sums up his whole philosophy. Horrified at the monotony, ugliness and vulgarity of the Industrial Revolution, he advocated a return to the medieval ideal of craftsmanship. Politically he was one of the founders of Socialism in England.

WILLIAM MORRIS TO PHILIP WEBB

Kelmscott House, Hammersmith
27 August 1894

My dear Fellow,
A traveller once entered a western hotel in America and went up to the clerk in his box (as custom is in that country) and ordered chicken for his dinner: the clerk, without any trouble in his face, put his hand into

his desk, and drew out a derringer, wherewith he covered the newcomer and said in calm historic voice: Stranger, you will not have chicken, you will have hash.

This story you seem to have forgotten. So I will apply it, and say that you will have the Kelmscott books as they come out. In short you will have hash because it would upset me very much if you did not have a share in my 'larx'.

As to the Olaf Saga, I had forgotten what you had had; chiefly I think because I did not prize the big-paper copies much. They were done in the days of ignorance, before the Kelmscott Press was, though hard on the time when it began.

You see as to all these matters I do the books mainly for you and one or two others; the public does not really care about them a damn – which is stale. But I tell you I *want* you to have them, and finally you *shall*.

Yours affectionately,
William Morris

Webb had remonstrated with Morris about his generosity in giving him copies of the books he printed at the Kelmscott Press which had been founded four years earlier to carry out Morris' ideas of typography and book-design. The books were printed by hand, using specially designed type, woodcut illustrations and fine paper. Its most famous publication was the works of Chaucer. Philip Webb, the designer of Morris' 'Red House', was a leader in the revolution in architecture, going back to function and abandoning such neo-classical features as stucco over the red-brick. The 'Olaf Saga' was one of the Old Norse sagas which Morris was among the first to appreciate and translate.

A tile with a drake designed by Philip Webb.

JEAN-FRANÇOIS MILLET TO ALFRED SENSIER

Barbizon, 1849

. . . My wish to paint a winter landscape has become an obsession . . .
I have plans for pictures of sheep as well. I have all kinds of plans.

If you could see how beautiful the forest is! I sometimes rush out into
it at dusk, after my day's work, and every time I come back feeling
crushed. Its calm and stateliness are terrifying, so much so that I catch
myself feeling really frightened. I don't know what those tatterdemalion
trees are saying to one another, but they're saying things we don't understand because we don't speak the same language, that's all. I don't think
they go in much for puns, though.

Tomorrow, Sunday, is the Barbizon fête. Every oven, stove and
chimney, every pot and pan, is so hard at work that it might be the day
before the marriage at Cana. Even the old curtain-rods are doing duty
as spits, and all the turkeys, geese, chickens and ducks that you saw in
such robust health are in process of being roasted, boiled, etc., etc., or
being made into pâtés the size of cart-wheels! In short, Barbizon is one
huge kitchen and the smell of it must be drifting far and wide.

*Jean-François Millet (1814–1875), a peasant boy from a village near Cherbourg,
went to Paris to study under the historical painter Delaroche, and began his
career with genre paintings and biblical scenes. In 1849 he settled at Barbizon, on
the outskirts of the Forest of Fontainebleau, where he led the life of a poor
cottager and painted his pictures of country scenes and activities.*

*Several other landscape painters came to live there concentrating on carefully
observed scenery, which they painted out of doors on the spot. They were among
the precursors of Impressionism.*

JEAN-FRANÇOIS MILLET TO ALFRED SENSIER

1860

My dear Sensier,
This is more or less what I wrote to Thoré about three of my pictures at
Martinet's:

In 'Woman who has just been drawing Water', I tried to show a
woman who is not a water-carrier, nor even a servant, but who had just

been drawing water for use in her own house, water to make soup for her husband and children; who should not seem to be carrying either more or less than the weight of the full buckets; I wanted her face to wear an expression of rustic kindliness, showing through the sort of grimace imposed upon it, as it were, by the weight dragging at her arms and the light that makes her screw up her eyes. I avoided, as usual, with a kind of horror, any suggestion of sentimentality. On the contrary, I wanted to show her occupied – with simplicity and good humour, not looking on it as a burden – in something which, like the other household tasks, is part of her day's work, the habit of a lifetime. I wanted also to convey an idea of the coolness of the well and to show, by its antique appearance, that many women before this one must have come to draw water from it.

In 'Woman Giving her Children a Meal', I wanted to suggest the idea of a brood of fledgelings being fed by their mother in the nest. The man goes to work to feed these creatures.

Millet took many of his subjects from peasant life. Of his painting 'Woman Giving her Children a Meal' he wrote, 'I wanted to suggest the idea of a brood of fledgelings being fed by their mother in the nest.'

In 'Sheep being sheared', I tried to express the kind of bewilderment and confusion that sheep feel when their thick wool has just been cut off, and the curiosity and stupefaction of those that have not yet been sheared, when their naked companions come back among them. I tried to make the place look like a peaceful, rustic dwelling, so that one can imagine the little field that lies behind it, and the poplars planted there to provide shade; in short to give it a long-standing air that calls forth memories.

I also told him, in case he might think it worth mentioning, that I try to make things look not as though they had been brought together pell-mell and for the occasion, but as though there were some indispensable, inevitable bond between them.

I would like the beings I depict to look as though they were pledged to their condition so that one cannot imagine it could occur to them to be anything different. People and objects must always be there for some purpose. I want to show lavishly and emphatically all that is necessary, for in my opinion things said feebly would be almost better left unsaid, because in that way they are somehow violated and spoilt, but I have the greatest horror of superfluities (however brilliant) and of padding, which can only distract the eye and weaken the effect.

I don't know whether all that was worth saying, but that was how it went. Tell me what you think. Will you come on Saturday, as you seemed almost to have decided? No news here. The children's whooping-cough seems to be calming down a little.

The family send you their greetings.

J.-F. Millet

JEAN-FRANÇOIS MILLET TO ALFRED SENSIER

Barbizon, 30 May 1863

The rumours about my 'Man with the Hoe' still seem very peculiar and am grateful to you for passing them on, since it gives me a fresh opportunity to wonder at the ideas attributed to me. In what club have my critics ever met me? Socialist! But really, I might well reply in the words of the countryman answering a charge made against him in his

Millet was accused of being a Socialist when he exhibited this picture, 'Man with the Hoe', but his belief in the dignity of peasant life was purely religious in origin.

native district, 'Folk in the village do be saying I be a Saint-Simonist; it bean't true, I doan't know what that be.'

Is it impossible simply to recognize that certain ideas may enter one's mind at the sight of a man destined to earn his living *by the sweat of his brow*? Some people tell me I deny the charms of the countryside; I see far more in it than charm, I see infinite splendours. I see, just as they do, the little flowers about which Christ said 'Verily I say unto you that Solomon in all his glory was not arrayed like one of these.'

I see very clearly the halos of the dandelions, and the sun, far away beyond the villages, suffusing the clouds with its glory. But I also see the steaming, straining horses on the plain, and the stony place where a man has been toiling and panting since morning, and now tries to straighten up for a short breather. The action is shrouded in splendours.

I have not invented all this, the expression 'the earth groans' is an old one.

'I see far more in [the countryside] than charm, I see infinite splendours' – '*Spring*' *was painted at Barbizon.*

My critics are, I suppose, men of learning and taste; but I cannot put myself in their shoes, and as all my life I have seen nothing but fields, I do my best to tell what I saw and felt when I was working there. There is plenty of opportunity for those who would like to do better, of course.

Millet's strong ethical and social convictions led him to depict his figures, such as 'The Sower' and 'The Gleaners', with an air of stately, even sublime dignity. Though attacked as a 'Socialist' he disclaimed any political allegiance – what he wanted to illustrate were the words 'in the sweat of thy face thou shalt eat thy bread', for only in them, as he wrote to his friend and biographer Sensier, did he find 'true humanity, great poetry'.

Gustave Courbet at his easel – a detail from his huge semi-allegorical painting, 'The Painter's Studio'.

'The Roebuck in the Forest' by Courbet. He describes this painting in a letter of 1866.

GUSTAVE COURBET TO URBAIN CUÉNOT, DESCRIBING HIS
PAINTING THE ROEBUCK IN THE FOREST

6 April 1866

It is a stream confined between rocks, with big trees; everything is pale
gold. Last winter I hired some roe deer and painted them in their cover;
in the middle a little doe is lying down, receiving her guests like a lady

in her drawing-room. Beside her is her buck . . . It's charming, and they have the finish of diamonds . . .

Gustave Courbet (1819–1877) was born at Ornans, near the Swiss frontier, came to Paris in 1840 and taught himself painting. His 'Stone Breakers' (1849) and 'Burial at Ornans' (1850), attacked by the traditionalists and hailed with delight by the younger painters, made him the recognized leader of the 'naturalistic' or 'realist' movement. He was a Bohemian, caustic of tongue, anti-academic, anti-intellectual, anti-clerical. He was involved in the revolution of 1848, and even more deeply in the Commune of 1871; he became Chairman of its Art Committee, and, in this capacity, was compelled to superintend the destruction of the column of Napoleon in the Place Vendôme. When the Commune was suppressed Courbet was arrested:

GUSTAVE COURBET TO MADAME JOLICLERC FROM SAINTE-PÉLAGIE PRISON

Paris, Autumn 1875

I have been plundered, ruined, traduced, dragged through the streets of Paris and Versailles, harrowed by stupidity and insults. I have rotted in solitary confinement where one loses one's reason and one's physical strength; I have slept on the ground, tossed among the scum of the earth in cells crawling with vermin, been taken from prison to prison, to hospitals with people dying all around, in police vans, in prisons too cramped for a man to enter, with a rifle or a revolver at my throat for four months.

But alas, I am not alone. There are two hundred thousand of us, dead and alive. Ladies, women of the working class, children of all ages, even nurslings, not to mention waifs, straying about Paris, fatherless and motherless, who are taken to prison every day in their thousands.

Nothing like it has been seen since the world began – no nation, no chronicle, no epoch has witnessed such slaughter, such vengeance.

Courbet had to pay a heavy fine. He went to Switzerland and lived by producing landscapes, dying there seven years later.

ÉDOUARD MANET TO HENRI FANTIN-LATOUR

Madrid, August (?) 1865

My dear fellow,

How I miss you here, and how delighted you would have been to see Velazquez, who in himself alone is worth the journey. The painters of all other schools, who surround him in the Madrid Gallery, and are very well represented there, all seem like *chiqueurs* [one who works from memory, without a model]. He is the painter of painters. He did not astonish me, but delighted me. The full-length portrait we have in the Louvre is not by him. Only the Infanta is beyond question. Here there is an enormous picture, full of little figures like those in the picture in the Louvre called 'Les Cavaliers'; but figures of men and women, perhaps better, and above all, quite untouched by the restorer. The background, the landscape, is by a pupil of Velazquez.

The most astonishing item among his splendid work, and perhaps the most astonishing ever painted, is the picture listed in the catalogue as 'Portrait of a famous Actor in the reign of Philip IV' [Pablillos de Valladolid, a court jester]. The background disappears; it is simply air that surrounds the man, dressed all in black and alive. And the 'Spinners', the fine portrait of Alonzo Cano, 'Las Meninas' [The Maids of Honour], another extraordinary picture! The philosophers, astonishing things! All the dwarfs; one in particular, seated, full face, his fists on his hips; just the painting for a real connoisseur. His magnificent portraits; one would like to mention everything; there are none but masterpieces. A portrait of Charles V, by Titian, which has a great reputation that must be deserved, and which I should certainly have thought good anywhere else, looks wooden here.

And Goya! The most curious after the master he imitated too closely, imitated in the most servile sense of the word. Great zest, though. There are two fine equestrian portraits by him in the gallery, in the style of Velazquez, but much inferior. What I have seen of his so far has not pleased me overmuch. In the next few days I am to see a magnificent collection of his work belonging to the Duke of Ossuna.

I am disconsolate; the weather looks very ugly this morning and I fear this evening's bull-fight, to which I have been looking forward, may

'Olympia.' When this painting was exhibited at the Salon of 1865 it caused such a scandal that Manet left France and went to Spain. The model was Victorine Meurand who had also posed for his painting 'Le Déjeuner sur l'herbe' which had caused a similar outcry two years earlier.

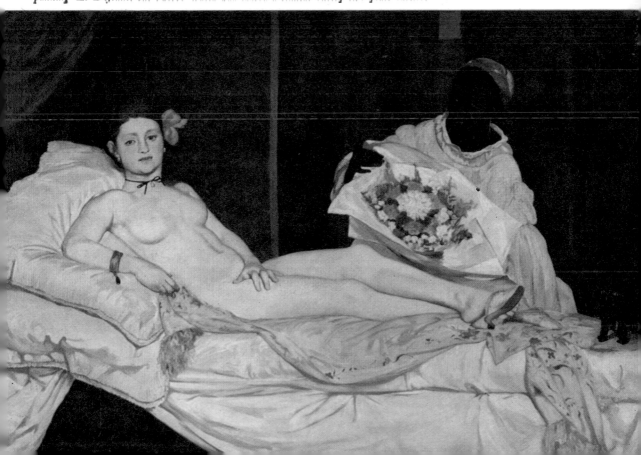

'Velazquez . . . in himself alone is worth the journey. . . . He is the painter of painters',
wrote Manet from Madrid. His painting, 'Les Petits Cavaliers', is a copy after Velazquez.

be postponed. Until when? Tomorrow I go to Toledo. There I shall
see Greco and Goya, who I am told are very well represented.

Madrid is a pleasant town, full of entertaining things. The Prado is
a charming public walk, crowded with pretty women, all in mantillas,
which gives it a very original appearance. In the streets one still sees
many national costumes; the toreros, too, have a curious street dress.

Farewell, my dear Fantin, I shake your hand and am yours very truly.

E. Manet

*Édouard Manet (1832–1883) had gone to Spain to gather new impressions after
the storm that had arisen over the exhibition of his 'Olympia' at the Salon of
1865. He had been the centre of a similar storm in 1863 over 'Le Déjeuner sur
l'herbe', which was partly responsible for the formation of the Salon des Refusés.
Zola was almost alone in defending him. Henri Fantin-Latour, another exhibitor
at the Salon des Refusés, was a close friend. He is best known for his flower-
paintings.*

ÉDOUARD MANET TO THÉODORE DURET

1875

My dear Duret,

I went to see Monet yesterday. I found him heart-broken and completely on the rocks. He asked me to find him someone who would take from ten to twenty of his pictures, at their choice, for 100 fr. apiece. Shall we do it between us, making 500 fr. each? Naturally, no one, least of all he, must know that it is we who are doing it. I had thought of a dealer, or of some collector or other; but it is just possible they might refuse.

Unfortunately one has to know as much about it as we do, in order to get an excellent bargain, in spite of one's natural reluctance, and at the same time do a service to a gifted man. Send me your answer as quickly as possible, or say when you could meet me.

Kind regards,
E. Manet

The Impressionist paintings sold at the Hôtel Drouot in Paris on 24 March 1875 had fetched deplorably low prices, particularly those by Claude Monet. Manet never called himself an Impressionist and never exhibited at their exhibitions.

ÉDOUARD MANET TO THE PRÉFET DE LA SEINE

April 1879

Monsieur,

I have the honour to submit for your distinguished approval the following plan for decorating the council chamber of the Municipal Council in the new Hôtel de Ville of Paris.

To paint a series of compositions representing – to use what has become a current phrase and which expresses my exact meaning – 'The Belly of Paris', with the different corporations displayed in their setting, the public and commercial life of the day. I would have Paris-Markets, Paris-Railways, Paris-Bridges, Paris-Underground, Paris-Races and Parks.

On the ceiling, a Gallery round which would circulate, with appropriate Movements, all the living men who, in the civilian element have helped or are now helping to make Paris great and rich.

> I beg to remain, etc.
> Edouard Manet.
> painter, born in Paris,
> 77, rue d'Amsterdam

The painter's offer to his native city was declined; indeed there is nothing to show that it was even answered. One of Manet's great dreams, cherished throughout his life, thus remained unfulfilled. The great figures of his own time were to include his friend Émile Zola, to whom he refers with the expression 'The Belly of Paris' ('Le Ventre de Paris') – the title of Zola's great novel.

'Portrait of Émile Zola.' The author is shown at work at his desk though the portrait was actually painted in Manet's studio. A reproduction of 'Olympia' has been pinned to the wall. Zola later described his sittings: 'I remember posing for hours on end . . . Now and again . . . I looked at the artist standing at his easel, his features taut, his eyes bright, absorbed in his work. He had forgotten me; he no longer realized that I was there.'

'. . . you would hardly believe, my dear fellow, how difficult it is to clap a solitary figure on a canvas and to concentrate the entire interest on that one solitary figure without it ceasing to be lively and full.' *Manet has succeeded admirably in this portrait of Antonin Proust which he discusses in his letter to the sitter.*

ÉDOUARD MANET TO ANTONIN PROUST

1880

For the last three weeks, my dear friend, your portrait has been in the Salon, badly hung on a piece of wall next to a door, and still more badly spoken of. Still, it is my lot to be abused, and I take it philosophically. But you would hardly believe, my dear fellow, how difficult it is to clap a solitary figure on a canvas and to concentrate the entire interest on that one solitary figure without it ceasing to be lively and full. To make two figures, which draw their attraction from their duality, is child's play by comparison. Ah! the portrait with the hat, where everything, people said, was blue! Well, I'm biding my time. I shall not see that day myself. But after my death people will realize that I saw things correctly and had the right ideas. Your portrait is an out-standingly sincere work. I remember as though it were yesterday the rapid, summary fashion in which I dealt with the glove of the ungloved hand. And when you said to me, at that very moment, 'Please, not another touch', I felt we were so perfectly attuned that I couldn't resist the impulse to embrace you. Ah! heaven send that no one takes it into his head later on to stick that portrait into a public collection! I have always had a horror of the mania for cramming works of art together without an inch between their frames, like the latest fads on the shelves of a fashionable shop. Well, time will show. Fate will decide.

Antonin Proust, politician and writer on art, was appointed Minister of Cultural Affairs in 1881. He was an intimate friend and patron of Manet and it was on his recommendation that the latter received the Légion d'honneur. 'So at last we have a Minister who realizes that people are painting in France', wrote Renoir in his letter of congratulation to Manet. He added, in contrast to the final words of Manet's own letter to Proust: 'I imagine that that Minister, who seems to be an intelligent, decent fellow, must know that his portrait is made for the Louvre and not for him.'

IMPRESSIONISM AND AFTER

CLAUDE MONET TO THE ART CRITIC ARSÈNE HOUSSAYE

2 June 1870

Monsieur Houssaye,

When I had the honour of calling upon you to ask your support in obtaining permission to work at the Salon, you advised me to move to Paris, where it would of course be easier for me to put my small talent to good use. My rejection at the Salon has determined me, for after that failure I can have no expectation of success at Le Havre. Gaudibert has again had the goodness to make it possible for me to settle here and to bring back my little family. Now we are settled and I am in very good fettle and full of the will to work, but alas, that fatal rejection is almost taking the bread out of my mouth, and in spite of my moderate prices, dealers and collectors turn their backs on me. It is particularly depressing to see how little interest is taken in any work of art that is not in public favour.

I have been thinking, and I hope you will excuse me, that since you already once found a picture of mine to your taste, you would perhaps look at the few paintings I have been able to save among the lot, for I thought you would be good enough to come to my help a little, for my circumstances are almost desperate, and the worst of it is that I cannot even go on working.

I need hardly assure you that I will do no matter what, and at whatever cost, to escape from such a situation and be able to begin work at once on my next Salon picture, so that the same thing shall not happen again.

Claude Monet (1840–1926), whose painting 'Impression: Sunrise' exhibited in 1874 gave a name to the movement of which he was the leading member, came from a grocer's family at Le Havre and had a hard struggle for the first twenty years of his career. By 1870 he had gained little recognition with either the Salon or the public. Arsène Houssaye was an influential art critic who had bought Monet's picture 'Camille' ('The Lady in the Green Dress'), a portrait of the artist's first wife, when it was exhibited at the Salon of 1866. Gaudibert had come to the artist's aid in 1868 by buying the canvases which had been seized by his creditors and by commissioning him to paint a portrait of Madame Gaudibert.

'The Luncheon' – an intimate domestic scene in which Monet portrays Camille, his first wife, and their son Je at table, while the maid and a visitor look on. It was painted in 1868.

CLAUDE MONET TO THE PUBLISHER GEORGES
CHARPENTIER

Vétheuil, 1878

I am literally penniless here, obliged to petition people, almost to beg for my keep, not having a penny to buy canvas and paints . . .

I had called on you this morning in the hope of arranging some small deal, no matter how small, so as not to go home with no money. I was unable to see you, and greatly regret it. I will send you a painting I think you will like. I ask you 150 francs for it, or, if that price seems to you too high, 100 francs, which I should be extremely grateful if you would send to me at Vétheuil, Seine-et-Oise. If the picture is not what you want, I will change it for another when I come back.

Thanking you in anticipation, your devoted
Claude Monet

P.S. I felt I could ask you this because for a long time you had led me to hope you would buy something from me.

I want to ask if you would be good enough to lend me or send me five or ten louis, I am in terrible difficulties at the moment.

I have been ten days in Paris without being able to raise a penny, and I cannot go back to the country, where my wife is very ill.

You would do me a very great service by giving that sum to the bearer and as soon as I return to Paris for good I will call on you and repay you either in painting or in money.

I hope you will not refuse me.

1878 was a particularly terrible year even for Monet who was again in desperate financial straits, while his wife was unwell and was to die the following year. In January he had rented a house at Vétheuil in a joint venture with Madame Hoschedé who with her six children came to live with the Monet family.

In 1880 Monet had a one-man show, and was at last acclaimed as a great painter. But success brought only an intensification of his inner struggle. In 1883 he went to live at Giverny on the borders of Normandy. Here he lived in his family circle (he married Madame Hoschedé in 1892), with occasional visits from close friends.

CLAUDE MONET TO HIS FRIEND GUSTAVE GEFFROY

Fresselines, 24 April 1889

I am distressed, almost discouraged, and fatigued to the point of feeling slightly ill. What I am doing is no good, and in spite of your confidence I am very much afraid that my efforts will all lead to nothing. Never have I been so unlucky with the weather. Never three suitable days in succession, so I have to be always making changes, for everything is growing and turning green. And I had dreamt of painting the Creuse just as we saw it!

In short, by dint of changes I am following Nature without being able to grasp her, and then there is the river that shrinks, swells again, green one day, then yellow, sometimes almost dry, and which tomorrow will be a torrent, after the terrible rain that is falling at the moment. In fact, I am very worried. Write to me; I have a great need of comfort, and you will readily understand that Rollinat is not the man to cheer me up. When I tell him of my worries all he can do is to go one better, and besides, while he knows the difficulties of his own art he does not realize what trouble I have to take in order to do what I do: he sees nothing in painting except the strange side of it.

Maurice Rollinat was a poet, author of 'Les Névroses'; he was living near Monet at the time, in a cottage on the banks of the Creuse.

CLAUDE MONET TO GUSTAVE GEFFROY

Giverny, 22 June 1890

I have gone back to some things that can't possibly be done: water, with weeds waving at the bottom. It is a wonderful sight, but it drives one crazy to try to paint it. But that is the kind of thing I am always tackling.

Monet had begun to paint the last of his great series of pictures on a single theme; after his 'Cathedrals', his 'Mornings on the Seine' and his 'Poplars', he was now painting the water-lilies on his pond. His friend Georges Clemenceau persuaded him to bequeath this series to the nation, and encouraged him to work, though his sight was beginning to fail:

'I have gone back to some things that can't possibly be done: water with weeds waving at the bottom.'
This painting, one of the famous water-lilies series, dates from 1918.

CLAUDE MONET IN OLD AGE

Colours no longer looked as brilliant to me as they used to do, I no longer painted shades of light so correctly. Reds looked muddy to me, pinks insipid, and the intermediate or lower notes in the colour scale escaped me. As for forms, I could see them as clearly as ever, and render them as decisively. At first I tried pertinacity. How many times I have

'The Water Garden at Giverny.' The water-lilies on this pool were to become the subject of Monet's last great series of paintings on a single theme.

remained for hours near the little bridge, exactly where we are now, in the full glare of the sun, sitting on my camp-stool, under my sunshade, forcing myself to resume my interrupted task and to recapture the freshness my palette had lost! A waste of effort. What I painted was more and more mellow, more and more like an 'old picture', and when the attempt was over and I compared it with what I used to do in the old days, I would fall into a frantic rage, and I slashed all my pictures with my penknife . . .

Though I remained insensitive to the subtleties and delicate gradations of colour seen at close quarters, my eyes at least did not deceive me when I drew back and looked at the subject in its broad lines, and this was the starting-point of new compositions. A very modest starting-point, to tell the truth. I distrusted myself, I was resolved to leave nothing to chance. Slowly I tried my strength in innumerable rough sketches which convinced me, in the first place, that the study of bright light was now, once and for all, impossible for me – but also reassured me by showing that while I could no longer go in for playing about with shades or for landscapes in delicate colours, I could see as clearly as ever when it came to vivid colours isolated in a mass of dark tones.

How was I to put this to use?

My intentions gradually became clearer. Ever since I entered my sixties I had had the idea of setting about a kind of 'synthesis' in each of the successive categories of themes that held my attention – of summing up in one canvas, sometimes in two, my earlier impressions and sensations. I had given up the notion. It would have meant travelling a great deal and for a long time, revisiting, one by one, all the places through which my life as a painter had taken me, and verifying my former emotions. I said to myself, as I made my sketches, that a series of general impressions, captured at the times of day when I had the best chance of seeing correctly, would not be without interest. I waited for the idea to consolidate, for the grouping and composition of the themes to settle themselves in my brain little by little, of their own accord; and the day when I felt I held enough cards to be able to try my luck with a real hope of success, I determined to pass to action, and did so.

PIERRE AUGUSTE RENOIR TO GEORGES CHARPENTIER

My dear friend,   *1877*

May I ask you if it is within possibility nevertheless, the sum of three hundred francs before the end of the month. If it is possible, I am truly grieved that it may be the last time and that I shall have nothing to write to you any more except commonplace, quite stupid letters, without asking you for anything because you will owe me nothing any longer except respect, that I am older than you, I do not send you my account because I have none.

Now, my dear friend, have the amiability to thank Madame Charpentier warmly on behalf of her most devoted artist and that I shall never forget that if one day I cross the tape that it is to her that I shall owe, for by myself I am certainly not capable of it. I would like to get there, so as to be able the sooner to procure her all my gratitude.

Pierre Auguste Renoir (1841–1919) spent four years of his youth painting pretty rococo pictures on porcelain, then studied under Gleyre, and achieved some success as a fashionable portrait painter. In 1868 he worked with Monet out of doors and his technique became more Impressionist. Charpentier, the recipient of Monet's rather similar letter, was a publisher and to a certain extent a patron of art. Renoir's portrait of Madame Charpentier and her children, painted in 1878, is now in the Metropolitan Museum of Art, New York, which paid 50,000 francs for it in his own lifetime. When asked how much he had been paid for it, he replied, 'Me! Three hundred francs and lunch.'

Like Monet, he lived to experience triumph; unlike Monet, he enjoyed it. He saw no reason for cutting himself off from commercial success merely because the Salon public was artistically prejudiced and ignorant:

PIERRE AUGUSTE RENOIR TO THE ART DEALER PAUL DURAND-RUEL

My dear Monsieur Durand-Ruel,   *Algiers, March 1881*

I have just been trying to explain to you why I send pictures to the Salon. In Paris there are scarcely fifteen people capable of liking a painter who doesn't show at the Salon. There are 80,000 who won't buy so much as a

'Moslem Feast in Algiers' was painted by Renoir on his first visit to 'this marvellous country' in 1881

nose from a painter who is not hung at the Salon. That's why I send in two portraits every year, little as that is. Besides, I do not want to fall in with the mania for believing that a thing is bad because of where it happens to be. In short, I don't want to waste time cherishing grudges against the Salon. I don't even want to seem to do so. In my opinion one should paint as well as possible, and that is all. Ah! If I were accused of neglecting my art, or sacrificing my opinions to idiotic ambition, I would understand my critics. But as that is not so, there is nothing they can reproach me with; on the contrary. At this moment, as always, I am concerned solely with doing good work. I want to paint stunning pictures that you can sell for very high prices. I shall manage it before long, I hope. I have been keeping away from all other painters, in the sun, to think things out. I believe I have come to an end and found what I wanted. I may be wrong, but it would very much surprise me. Be patient for a little longer, and I hope I shall soon prove to you that one can show at the Salon and still do good painting.

So please plead my cause with my friends. I send to the Salon for purely commercial reasons. Anyhow, it's like with certain medicines. If it does no good, it does no harm.

I think I'm quite fit again now. I'm going to be able to work hard and make up for lost time.

Renoir returned to North Africa the following year and painted 'The Stairway, Algiers'.

At which point I wish you excellent health. And a lot of rich collectors. But keep them till I get back. I shall stay here another month. I don't want to leave Algiers without bringing back something from this marvellous country.

A thousand greetings to my friends and to you.

Renoir

PIERRE AUGUSTE RENOIR TO PAUL DURAND-RUEL

Naples, 21 November 1881

Dear Monsieur Durand-Ruel,

I have been meaning to write to you for a long time, but I wanted to send you a mass of pictures as well. But I am still bogged down in experiments – a malady. I'm not satisfied, so I clean things off, again and again. I hope the mania is coming to an end, that is why I am giving you this sign of life. I do not think I shall bring back very much from my travels. But I think I shall have made progress, which always happens after experimenting for a long time. One always comes back to one's first love, but with a note added. Anyhow, I hope you will forgive me if I don't bring you back a great deal. Besides, you'll see what I shall do for you in Paris.

I am like a child at school. The new page is always going to be neatly written, and then pouf! . . . a blot. I'm still making blots . . . and I am 40 years old. I went to look at the Raphaels in Rome. They are very fine and I ought to have seen them earlier. They are full of skill and wisdom. He didn't try to do the impossible, like me. But his work is fine. I prefer Ingres for oil painting. But the frescoes are admirable in their simplicity and nobility.

I take it you are well, as usual, and your little family too. But I shall be seeing you soon, for Italy is very fine. But Paris . . . Ah! Paris . . .

I am beginning something. I won't tell you what, because then I should spoil it. I have my superstitions.

A thousand greetings,

Renoir

Madame Misia Sert was painted by Renoir no less than eight times. An invitation from him to come and sit for her fourth portrait appears on the following page.

PIERRE AUGUSTE RENOIR TO MADAME MISIA SERT

3 July 1906

Come, and I promise that in the 4th portrait I will try to make you even more beautiful. I myself am well, and I shall be even better if you can come and see me at Essoyes this summer. Meanwhile I shall work with an enchanting model sent to me by Valoton [*sic*]. So now, for writing to me: Essoyes – Aube. I will do my best to show you some amusing things and we will eat as well as we can.

'I want to paint stunning pictures that you can sell for very high prices.' Renoir achieved such a combination in his portrait of Madame Charpentier and her children. It was sold during his lifetime for 50,000 francs.

Madame Joseph Durand-Ruel, the daughter-in-law of the famous art dealer who did so much to help Renoir and the other Impressionists. This painting of 1911 shows the artist's increasing interest in colour, line and pattern for their own sakes.

Many of Renoir's later paintings are of women—many of them nudes. He painted Madame Sert eight times in different gowns and poses; he would beg her to pull down the top of her dress – 'Lower, lower, I implore you – why for heaven's sake don't you show your bosom? – it's a crime!'

In his last years Renoir was crippled by arthritis but continued to paint with brushes strapped to his wrists. He died in 1919.

AUGUSTE RODIN TO THE CHAIRMAN OF THE MONUMENTS
COMMITTEE

1885

My dear Chairman,

I have just been rereading a note in the *Patriote de Calais* which repeats, more or less, the criticism already put forward, but which would emasculate my work; 'the heads should form a pyramid' (the method of Louis David) 'instead of a cube or a straight line'; this is simply the School laying down the law to me; *I am diametrically opposed to this principle*, which has prevailed in our period since the beginning of the century; it is diametrically opposed to the previous great periods of art, and the works conceived in this spirit are cold, lifeless, and conventional.

2. Eustache de Saint-Pierre seems to the critic to be in the presence of the king; so what are the men behind him supposed to be doing? No, he is leaving the town and going down towards the camp; this is what gives the group the appearance of advancing, of movement. Eustache is the first to begin going down, and for my lines he has to be like that.

3. The monument is to be in a garden or in a monument designed by an architect. *It is to be in the middle of a square.*

The one who has lost heart and is plunged deep in thought alone may be altered; if you can keep it to that, my group is saved. These Gentlemen do not know that this is a model to a scale of one third, not a consultation with a view to beginning the work all over again.

In Paris I am the antagonist of this theatrical and School art. That would be wanting to make me the follower of people whose conventional art I despise.

The subject of this letter is Rodin's sculpture group 'The Burghers of Calais', which had been severely criticized on various grounds. Rodin did not want it to stand on a pedestal, as was customary, but on the ground, in a public garden, so that the present-day burghers could meet their forebears face to face.

Auguste Rodin (1840–1917) came from a family in very modest circum-stances and when he failed to gain admission to the École des Beaux-Arts – his work was already anti-academic – he had to support himself by working as a sculptor's assistant. At the age of twenty-four he sent his 'Man with a Broken

Nose' to the Salon, but it was rejected on account of its 'lack of moral elevation'. He visited Italy in 1876 and was influenced by Michelangelo. But at the same time he was closely in touch with the Impressionists and declared in a letter to Monet that he was grateful to painting for helping him to understand light, clouds and the sea, while in his drawings he tried to capture movements and gestures in all their changing aspects. Rodin was also grouped with the Impressionists in the public mind by his opposition to academicism.

He failed to win over the town council of Calais to his views on the 'Burgher' group, just as he had failed at Nancy over the 'Claude Lorrain' statue, and was to fail many times subsequently. In the private field, however, his portrait busts were greatly admired and much in demand.

'The monument is to be in a garden . . .'. Rodin's famous sculpture group, 'The Burghers of Calais', now stands in the garden before the Town Hall.

'Portrait Bust of Georges Clemenceau.' Rodin's portrait busts were much in demand.

AUGUSTE RODIN TO CAPTAIN BIGAND-KAIRE

October/December 1900

I have to tell you, my friend, that the moral result of my exhibition is very fine, and that as to money, I shall cover my expenses. I have sold 200,000 francs' worth and I hope even a little more. And some commissions as well. Nearly all the galleries bought from me: Philadelphia, 'La Pensée'; Copenhagen, 80,000 francs' worth, for a room to myself in their gallery; Hamburg, Dresden, Budapest, etc. . . . Not many Americans, not many English, but a great many Germans at my exhibition. So you see things always turn out unexpectedly. Not much gate-money, on which I was relying; a great many purchases. Of the 200,000 francs, I deduct $\frac{1}{3}$ for expenses, marble, bronze; that leaves 140,000; I have 150,000 francs of expenses. That, my friend, very pleased, is the news I have for you, hoping to see you soon.

Aug. Rodin

Rodin read a great deal; literature provided ideas and the stimulus for many of his works, such as the unfinished 'Gate of Hell' which was inspired by Dante's 'Inferno'. In his will he counsels the young to bring their work to perfection like honest craftsmen, as the old masters did, and love the labour involved. One of his last letters is to the Belgian poet Émile Verhaeren, who was himself involved in modernist movements in art and who died in 1916:

AUGUSTE RODIN TO ÉMILE VERHAEREN

My great Poet,
Whom I love in his strength, who nourishes me, who says things that are true.

Like a ploughman, your plough, your thought, flings off the clods to right and left of the wound, from the edges; – you bring fertility, your seed is genuine. I express it badly, but you understand rightly . . . I have so many worries. The seed, the evil seed, is upon me . . .

Like one who invents his life and, finding it difficult after having completed it, discovers the secret of it in the fine precepts we were taught in our catechism, but at which we used to laugh . . . This assembly of precepts discourses with me familiarly, like wise friends, as I lie in bed. How my whole life, even in its best moments, falls short of this sweetness . . . This mountain whence the men of ancient time reveal the wise life to me, and my mistakes, all caused by my stupid vanity, by foolish ambition. – Where the honey of wisdom shows up my idiotic mistakes. Stern, gentle reflections these great ones are putting forward for me just now. Punishment must sweep your mind clear, to prepare it for the fine reflections in the good books . . . What sweetness there is in learning one's errors, even if irreparable, but one's errors!

143

'Regent's Park, London. Primrose Hill' was finished by Pissarro in France.

CAMILLE PISSARRO TO HIS SON LUCIEN

Éragny, 26 April 1892

My dear Lucien,

Yes, I should certainly have wasted time if I had left with you. Here I have been able to make some good spring studies in oils, and managed to finish my 'Cow-girl' and my 'Seated Woman' and my 'London Park', Primrose Hill. I think these pictures have improved a great deal from the point of view of unity. How different from the studies! I am more than ever in favour of taking one's impression from memory; it is less the actual thing – vulgarity disappears, leaving only an aura of truth glimpsed, sensed. To think that this is not understood, so that my anxiety for the future continues as before, despite the success of the

'Kew Green' – another of Pissarro's London views.

exhibition. – I have no news from Paris about my collectors. Can it be the fear of dynamite that is freezing them?

Camille Pissarro (1831–1903), the son of a Jewish merchant in the West Indies, came to Paris in 1855. He painted landscapes and peasant subjects and became the friend of Monet, Cézanne and Gauguin. In 1874 he exhibited in the first Impressionist exhibition. He adopted the Pointillist technique in 1884, but soon abandoned it. Less of a devotee to theory than Seurat, he remained consistent in the Impressionist ideal of fidelity to visual appearance. Towards the end of his life he lived at his estate at Éragny. His five sons all became painters or craftsmen. Lucien, the eldest, finally settled in England where he founded the Éragny Press designing many of the woodcut illustrations for it himself. This letter shows Pissarro's ideas changing yet again – he was constantly in search of new means of expression – away from painting on the spot and towards a more con-sidered composition.

The reference to dynamite is an allusion to the recent anarchist outrages – a bomb had just been thrown at the Café Véry – and to the Ravachol trial, which was the great topic of the day. Pissarro had contributed to a collection on behalf of the children of the anarchists who had been arrested.

CAMILLE PISSARRO TO HIS SON LUCIEN

Éragny, 26 July 1893

Georges tells me Epping is not beautiful. Bah! One can do such lovely things with so little. Subjects that are too beautiful end by appearing theatrical – take Switzerland, for example. Think of all the beautiful little things old Corot did at Gisors: two willows, a little water, a bridge, like the picture in the Universal Exhibition. What a masterpiece! Blessed are they who see beautiful things in humble places where other people see nothing! Everything is beautiful, all that matters is to be able to interpret. And from your description it seems to me to be very interesting . . .

CAMILLE PISSARRO TO HIS SON LUCIEN

Éragny, 15 September 1893

My dear Lucien,

Heavens, how the money runs away!! I have not much left. I only hope Durand, who has a knack of realizing when one needs him, won't start playing me any low tricks . . . I am waiting impatiently for the moment to go to Paris about it. Chène, the dealer in the Rue de la Paix, is very keen on the idea of making a bargain between me and the jeweller, Vever. He is a big speculator in the 1830 school, who has made big sums at that game; it seems he's within an inch of coming to the point. But the Chicago Exhibition, which he didn't manage to avoid, has been a colossal disaster. I'm afraid that may cool him off. It's most un-fortunate about that Chicago folly. Who the devil wants to go among those pork-butchers???

'Blessed are they who see beautiful things in humble places.' *The Siesta, Éragny.*

You remember Monet told me Montaignac would return to the charge. Not likely! He doesn't stir; to be sure, he represents Sutton, the big American dealer who has a hundred and twenty Monets. Unfortunately he doesn't like my things. He said so to Duret, and to Monet as well. And yet, why not? He may come round, and be even more enthusiastic by way of reaction. All the same I'm worried. At Chène's gallery I was introduced to an American dealer who won't touch anything except the 1830s. He admitted to me that there had been a great step forward.

'Well then!' said Chène, 'get started while it's not too expensive!'

147

'Oh, we don't feel so confident as all that', said the dealer. 'There are too many Monets on Sutton's hands. If he doesn't bring off a good sale in the near future, it may prove to have been a bad investment!'

Sutton has gone into competition with Durand, they're fighting each other at our expense. I only learn of these things in snatches which worry me a great deal. Oh well, not being a speculator, I tell myself to leave it to luck!

The weather today is frightful, rain and wind. You must be having the same at Epping, it's a pity. It had been so fine for the last few days and I had begun to grind away from nature. This is infuriating, for it's the loveliest time of the year, September and October. I can't stand the summer any more, with its heavy, monotonous green, its dry distances, where everything can be seen, the torment of the great heat, prostration and somnolence. Artistic sensations revive in September and October . . . but then it rains and blows!

'Sutton' is James F. Sutton, one of the founders of the American Art Association, who had invited Durand-Ruel, in 1884, to organize his first exhibition in New York.

CAMILLE PISSARRO TO HIS SON LUCIEN

Paris, 26 April 1900

My dear Lucien,

Decidedly, we are at cross-purposes. What's all this you tell me about the modern movement, commercialism, etc., etc.? It bears no relation to our conception of art, at any rate here. You know quite well that just as William Morris had an influence on commerce in England, so the real artists, who are looking for something, have had, and will have, a certain influence on commercial art. We cannot prevent this stupid vulgarization. They even go to the point of making colour prints for grocers from some of Corot's figures . . . that is an absolute fact. Oh yes, I am well aware that turning to the Greeks and the primitives is a reaction against commercialism. That is where the error lies. Trade serves those up to us as readily as anything else; so it is no use. Wouldn't it be better to steep ourselves in genuine nature again? I do not consider in the least that we are making a mistake, that we should turn to the steam-engine and follow the general public. No, a thousand times no! We are here to point the way! According to you, the remedy lies with the Italian primitives. According to me, that is an error . . . the remedy is to be found in nature, more than ever. Let us follow what we consider to be the proper aim, we shall see who is right. After all, money is a fragile thing; let us earn some of it, since we must, but let us keep to our role. . . .

CAMILLE PISSARRO TO HIS SON LUCIEN

Paris, 8 May 1903

This Mr Dewhurst has not understood the Impressionist movement in the very least. All he sees in it is a technical method, and he mixes up the names, he regards Jongkind as inferior to Boudin. A pity. He also says that before going to London we [Monet and I] knew nothing whatsoever about light; but we have studies that prove the contrary. He omits the influence of Claude Lorrain, Corot, all the 18th-century painters, Chardin most of all. But what he fails to realize is that while Turner and Constable were of service to us, they confirmed our suspicion that those painters had not understood *The Analysis of Shadows*, which in the case of Turner are always a deliberate effect, a plain dark patch. As to the division of tones, Turner confirmed for us its value as a method, but not as a means of accuracy or truth to nature. In any case, the 18th century was our tradition. It seems to me that Turner, too, had looked at Claude Lorrain, I am even inclined to think there is a picture by Turner, 'Sunset', hung side by side with a Claude! That's typical. . . . What do you think of it? He has some cheek, has Mr Dewhurst.

The English painter Wynford Dewhurst was writing a book (eventually published in 1904) called 'Impressionist Painting, its Genesis and Development'. Pissarro had just seen extracts from it published in 'The Studio'. Turner had asked in his will that his 'Sun rising through Vapour' (1807) and 'Dido building Carthage' (1815) should be hung next to two paintings by Claude Lorrain in the National Gallery.

GEORGES SEURAT TO MAURICE BEAUBOURG

August 1890

... To end with, I will give you the aesthetic and technical memorandum that concludes M. Christophe's book, and which is by me. *I am changing it a little, not having been quite understood by the printer.*

AESTHETICS:

Art is harmony.

Harmony is the analogy of contraries, the analogy of similarities, of *tone*, of *colour*, of *line*, considered from the angle of the dominant and under the influence of lighting in cheerful, tranquil or melancholy combinations.

The contraries are:

For tones, a $\begin{cases} \text{brighter} \\ \text{paler} \end{cases}$ for a darker one.

For colour, the complementaries, i.e. a certain red contrasted with its complementary, etc. (red-green; orange-blue; yellow-mauve).

For lines, those that make a right-angle.

Cheerfulness of *tone* is the bright dominant; of *colour*, the warm dominant; of *line*, lines above the horizontal.

Tranquillity of tone is equality of dark and pale; of colour, of warm and cold, and the horizontal for lines.

Melancholy of tone is the cold dominant, and of line, the downward direction.

TECHNIQUE:

Taking for granted the phenomena of the duration of the impression made by light on the retina.

Synthesis is the necessary resultant. The means of expression is the optical mingling of tones, colours (localized colour and the colour of the lighting, sun, oil lamp, gas, etc.), that is to say of the lights and their reactions (shadows) according to the laws of the *contrast* of graduation, irradiation.

The frame should be in the harmony contrasting with that of the tones, colours and lines of the picture.

Georges Seurat (1859–1891) was the great theorist of the Neo-Impressionists. Pointillism (or Divisionism) was his invention, though in the early days Pissarro was an equally ardent practitioner. It was to be a modern synthesis of methods based on a scientific foundation, taking its inspiration from Chevreul, the chemist, who had been carrying out research on colour contrasts, and from James Maxwell, the physicist, with his theories on the nature of light. The idea was to break up the colours into specks and leave it for the eye of the beholder to reassemble them.

'M. Christophe' is Seurat's biographer Jules Christophe. Unable to understand Seurat's theory he had asked the artist to write down the principal points himself for inclusion in the book.

Pointillism was the invention of Georges Seurat. This painting, 'Sunday Afternoon on the Island of La Grande Jatte', necessitated numerous preparatory studies and drawings and took him two years to paint.

HENRI DE TOULOUSE-LAUTREC TO HIS COUSIN MADELEINE
TAPIÉ

Nice, 1881

I have as my neighbour a Mademoiselle Lecouteur De Jessey. She is
of very ripe years. Facing us are an Armenian man and a young Russian
doctor who is the nephew (and heir presumptive) of M. Nanikoff. Most
of the others are old, ugly Englishwomen. I may mention old Captain
Campbell (AN OLD ACQUAINTANCE), the Misses Parsons –
Americans whose acquaintance we were privileged to make last year –
and Mrs Elliot who (I learnt later) is about to celebrate (hush) her 50th
birthday and looks 30 at the very most. She recently married a Member
of Parliament, M. Isaac.

19 January – Forgive me, my dear cousin. Sloth, and even more the
bad weather, have restrained my hand!! Rain, flic, flac, filth, mud,
boredom, the Eternal Father has granted us all this in profusion.
Disgusting, isn't it?

To sum up. I have seen the Suermondts, as pleasant as ever . . . It
makes me all the more sorry they are not at this hotel. Here it's rather
gloomy, I miss my Dutchman!!! To rely on him to cheer one up – that
gives you the key to the rest. At table I watch the Armenian and pass
the mustard to Mlle Lecouteur. It's almost as eventful as a convent. M.
Suermondt returned yesterday, from his house. He came here and was
kind enough to give me some encouragement. Mademoiselle (you know
she doesn't want us to call her Miss) came too. She had the good idea of
coming late. So I was unable to horrify her with my works. The exhibition has opened and I have done a portrait of Dash. The sitting was
amusing because he got angry with Eugène, who had been told to keep
him in position.

Frau Bittmann is talking drivel, she is determined, 'Monsieur lé
Gonde', to push her daughter at us. Luckily Mamma is determined to
refuse.

Phew! . . .

This is how it happened. M. Feltissoff (M. Nanikoff's nephew) has
a brother who got married yesterday evening. To mark the occasion he

gave a little family party consisting of Mme Viroulet, M. Lévi, M. and Mlle Firtains, M. and Mme Isaac, M. Louis and M. ——, plus Eugène. Having, as I say, cooked this up for after dinner, they titivated themselves up to the nines. When we left the table, they came to take our places. I was in the gallery, feeling pretty bored, when Mlle Lecouteur came, very amiably (if I'd only known) to invite me to join in their innocent pastimes. I went across and sat down beside a very tall and very ugly Miss who arrived two days ago, when Adolphe came to say a gentleman wanted to speak to me (if I'd only known!). I rushed out to the hall, but he drew me into the dining-room. I was scarcely inside when M. Feltissoff planted a nosegay in my buttonhole (his own, if you please) and Madame, placing me on her right, had 4 different glasses brought to me. I protested at first, but M. Feltissoff would have none of it. So I began, a little at first . . . Tlac. Good, isn't it? Anyhow, as you know, only the first glass needs an effort . . . It was going very well . . . As for them, they had a good start on me and were becoming affectionate. We drank the health of the bride and bridegroom. Ah, Madame Viroulet!!! At that moment feelings were at such a pitch that M. Morgan and M. Virtan kissed Mme Viroulet. Eugène was capering like a monkey, M. Lévi was shouting hip, hip, hip, Hurrah!!! and as for me, I had a frightful headache.

After a short time I went to bed, very shamefaced. In a bad way. I felt quite off colour!!! I was beginning to wonder whether it would last long, when all of a sudden a tremendous Bea aou rra! put an end to my uncertainty. No need to tell you any more! I'll spare you the compliments Mamma lavished on me.

Wednesday, 26 January. After one unsuccessful experiment they have paid in a few more sesterces and there is to be a ball this evening. I'll try to put you in the picture, 5.30 p.m.

Dinner at 5.30. People were nervous, thinking of the great event. The table was removed at once, leaving only one end of it for the buffet. I watched these preparations in the company of a placid Englishman who was smoking a pipe. They nailed down the oilcloth and scrubbed it. We went off to titivate. You can imagine how serious it was when I tell you I looked almost clean.

Came down. Everyone still in the lounge. There were two young Englishmen, who have the room next to ours, who were superb, their two sisters, who resemble umbrellas were there as guests, dressed in pink, with a little red-haired Miss in blue. It's a type I've tried to show on horseback, but I haven't succeeded.

I went to the gallery. The musicians were there, a piano (belonging to the hotel) a cello and a violin. (Gabriel, why weren't you there.) Then the male guests arrived. There were two officers, one of whom was here two years ago. Dzin, boum, boum, the ball began, with four young ladies to dance. People were beginning to mutter that it wasn't worth it (two young English ladies staying at the hotel, the most enthusiastic dancers, were ill) when a flock of innocent beauties arrived on the scene, we may mention in passing Mlle Lecouteur (who has completed her 35th year), Miss Armitèze [*sic*] (a female chimpanzee, sister of the clergyman, 50 years in the fog) and Miss Ludlou [*sic*] (who laughs like a hen and is midway between the two). The first two had opened their hearts and were revealing a fine set of violin strings. Dzin, boum, boum . . . It filled up with two or three Misses and two young widows in black satin (where will mourning perch next!). Dzin, boum, boum. (Now this is for me), Mme V., in black velvet (what d'you think of that?) and M. Fitissoff running to a corner near the buffet with the two Captains, Morgan and Campbell. I was congratulating myself on my position when Attchoo!!! AAAAt!!! choo!!! Everyone began to sneeze. The dancing young ladies struggled desperately not to sneeze; their partners likewise; one man simply abandoned his partner and went off to a corner for a quarter of an hour. Old Captain Campbell was convinced he had a bad cold, so was Monsieur Lévy [*sic*]. Captain Morgan was just assuring us that he wasn't in the least under the general influence, when . . .

It was a magnificent sight.

Henri de Toulouse-Lautrec-Monfa (1864–1901) came from one of the most ancient families of the French aristocracy. He was sixteen years old when he wrote the above account and was already aware that he was doomed to be a cripple for the rest of his life. He had been drawing continuously from an early age, mainly hunting scenes and horses to begin with, and had already started painting. Scorned by his father and feeling an outcast in the society into which he was born, Toulouse-Lautrec found his true home in the Bohemian milieu of the Paris music-halls, cafés and brothels. These inspired the lithographs, posters and paintings which brought him such fame and established his reputation. In 1899 his health completely broke down and he had to seek refuge in a clinic, and he died at the age of thirty-eight. This extract is taken from a diary he kept while convalescing at Nice after his two accidents. He gave it the title of 'Cahier de Zig-zags' and dedicated it to his cousin Madeleine Tapié to amuse her with his lively descriptions of incidents and impressions of his stay with his mother at a hotel in the South of France.

A page from the sixteen-year-old Toulouse-Lautrec's 'Cahier de Zig-zags' with his sketch of the two Englishwomen 'who resemble umbrellas'.

MAX LIEBERMANN TO ALFRED LICHTWARK

Wannsee, 5 June 1911

Dear Friend,

Your letter of 31 May gave me special pleasure, it arrived in the morning and I meant to answer it at once, that very evening. But the evenings in the garden are so lovely that I could not bring myself to sit down at my desk, and so a week has gone by and I am using the peace of the second Sunday – even my good Luise, '*le coeur simple*', is still asleep – to do in the morning what has become impossible in the evenings simply because of you (for your active co-operation in the garden has made me so much fonder of it than before).

Well, as regards Christ, or rather Jesus in the Temple. I painted it at Munich between the end of December 1878 and April 1879. I came to Munich from Venice, where I had spent two months, meaning to stay only a few days, but the few days developed into six years. The idea of the picture goes back to 1876, as can be seen from a great many drawings in my sketchbooks – which I'll show you sometime if you come to Berlin. Then, in 1877, I painted the study of the Amsterdam synagogue which Schulte now owns, and while in Venice I did one of the local synagogue, a 16th-century building, which can be seen in the picture on the stairs. The Temple picture I began, as I have said, at Munich, and it was the first thing I painted there. I took my models out of the Christian hospitals at Munich, partly because Jews will seldom sit for artists and partly for another reason that has influenced my choice of models ever since my young days. It seems to me that the Jewish type is too marked, it leads one astray into caricature – a mistake Menzel seems to me to have committed. I think I made the same remark to you many years ago, when I was to have painted Mommsen for you. Mommsen was too much the German professor out of the *Fliegende Blätter*, who's always losing his umbrella. I painted Jesus from an Italian model. I have come to the conclusion that Rembrandt's models were mostly Christians. His accentuation of the spiritual aspect led to the assumption that for the most part he painted Jews, for instance the picture called 'The Jewish Bride' is done from Hendrickje and his son Titus.

Liebermann's painting, 'Jesus in the Temple', made him famous in a few hours when it was first exhibited – it also caused an outcry.

Rembrandt painted the spirit of the Jews, whereas Menzel reproduced their outward appearance; just as Leibl and Defregger did with the Tyrolese. The former represented them like a painter, i.e. from within, and the other, Defregger, had a literary, external approach to them.

I expect I have told you how that picture, which came before the jury of the exhibition at 10 o'clock in the morning, had made me famous by evening, so that I was allowed to join Gedon, Lenbach and Wagmüller – the gods, in fact – in the 'Allotria'; how Zügel declared that no such masterpiece had been painted at Munich for fifty years, that the Prince Regent wanted the picture removed from the exhibition, that there was a two-day debate on it in the Bavarian Parliament (and it was entirely thanks to the then leader of the Centre party that I was not crucified); how I got to know Leibl through that picture and how – Lenbach having advised me to seek refuge in flight from the rage of the mob – I went to Dachau and rediscovered it for painting. *Habent fata sua tabulae.* Stöcker asserted that it was that picture that started him on his anti-Jewish campaign, and my brethren in the faith made me pay dearly for this, refusing for at least 15 years to buy any more of my work. The most disgusting newspaper feud broke out over it, and while I, sickened by all the hubbub which now, when looking at the picture, seems almost incredible, resolved never again to paint a biblical subject, the Jesus became the starting-point for the new religious painting . . .

Max Liebermann (1847–1935), the son of a wealthy Jewish industrialist, was born in Berlin. He studied under Munkacsy in Paris and in 1874 went to Barbizon where he lived for some time and was much influenced by Millet. 'Jesus in the Temple' was painted immediately after his return to Germany in 1878. This letter, written thirty years after the event, implies that he was more interested in the subject-matter than in technique. Later, however, he painted in an increasingly Impressionist manner and became the leading exponent of Impressionism in Germany. He also owned a fine collection of Impressionist works and wrote a book on Degas. In 1899 he became the first President of the recently launched splinter movement ('Sezession') in Berlin. As a Jew his works were later removed from public galleries by the Nazis. The 'Jesus in the Temple', formerly in the Kunsthalle, Hamburg, was sold in 1941 and its present whereabouts is unknown.

EDVARD MUNCH TO HIS AUNT KAREN BJØLSTAD

Berlin, 1903

There was a continuous invasion of Christiania Bohemians this evening, drinking themselves into a stupor and interrupting my work. Some of them realized, I noticed, that I positively must get away from Christiania and most of the people there – and break off altogether any connection with the circle, headed by X, who have treated me with such fiendish

'Self-portrait between Clock and Bed.' This self-portrait was painted by Edvard Munch in 1940 – four years before his death.

injustice and embittered my life. It is clear to me, as well, that I must take definite steps to rid myself of the neurasthenia caused by this evil woman's years of persecution. I can see now that all these violent scenes are only the unhealthy outcome of that long torment. I am going to find somewhere absolutely quiet, so that I can paint in peace.

I am still getting the most flattering letters from Germany – in Weimar they are doing everything to get me back and there are already two commissions there. In addition I have been commissioned to paint a portrait in Chemnitz, Saxony. But I am not going before my nerves have settled down.

Greetings to Inger and Laura.

Your affec. Edvard Munch

Edvard Munch (1863–1944), the Norwegian painter and graphic artist, is writing to his aunt under severe mental stress, and at a time when he was a prey to an acute persecution mania. His condition was aggravated by the fact that the 'evil woman' with whom he had had an affair some years previously, had obliged him to make regular payments to her.

The 'Christiania Bohemians' were a group of Norwegian artists and writers among whom Munch had spent his early years as an artist. His strange, haunting pictures, with their melancholy eroticism and preoccupation with death had scandalized the Norwegian critics. As a result Munch went abroad, to Paris, and then to Germany where he chiefly lived from 1892 to 1908. It was there that his work was most appreciated and his artistic reputation flourished. In 1908 his mental troubles cumulated in a physical and nervous breakdown which took him into a Danish nursing home. After his recovery, he was given a place of distinction at the 'Sonderbund' exhibition at Cologne, being classed as one of the four pioneers of modern art, the others being Cézanne, Van Gogh and Gauguin. His importance was recognized in his own country when he was commissioned to paint a series of murals for the University of Oslo. He had a great influence on the Expressionist painters and is now regarded as the leading Scandinavian painter of his time.

Munch never married and the only intimate writings we possess of his are his letters to his family, in particular his aunt and his two sisters, to whom he was deeply attached.

PAUL GAUGUIN TO GEORGES DANIEL DE MONFREID

Tahiti, November 1895

My dear Daniel,

At the moment of receiving your kind letter I have not yet touched a brush, except to paint a glass window in my studio. I had to stop over in Papeete in temporary quarters and take a decision; finally to have a big Tahitian hut built for me in the country. A magnificent site, by the way, in the shade, at the roadside, with a stunning view of the mountains behind me. Imagine a huge bird-cage with bamboo bars and a roof of coconut-thatch, divided into two parts by my old studio curtains. One part serves as the bedroom, with very little light, so as to be cool. The other part has a big window overhead, to make a studio. On the floor there are some mats and my old Persian rug; the whole place is adorned with pieces of material, curios and drawings.

You see I am not too much to be pitied for the moment.

Every night my bed is invaded by little madcap girls; last night I had three of them at work. I am going to stop this giddy life, take a serious woman into the house and work steadily, more especially as I feel I'm in form and I think I can do better things than before.

My former wife got married while I was away and I have been obliged to cuckold her husband, but she can't live with me, though she did run back to me for a week . . .

Paul Gauguin (1848–1903), whose romantic life influenced the following generation almost as much as his painting, was the son of a French journalist. His mother was a Peruvian of Spanish descent and he spent some of his early years at Lima. Later he was a pupil at the French Naval Academy, went to South America sailing before the mast, became a successful stock-broker, collected Impressionist pictures, and took to painting at the age of thirty. In 1883 he gave up his financial career and devoted himself to art. After a few years in Paris he retired to Britanny, and began his new style of painting. After staying with Van Gogh at Arles, he left Europe for Tahiti, declaring 'Je veux aller chez les sauvages'; he was then forty-three years old. In 1893 he returned to France, but went back to Tahiti after two years.

Daniel de Monfreid was a minor artist who had known Gauguin since his early days as a full-time artist in Montparnasse. He had, said Gauguin's daughter, 'a particular pleasure in arranging other people's affairs'.

PAUL GAUGUIN TO GEORGES DANIEL DE MONFREID

14 February 1897

You will shortly be receiving several pictures: what with my physical and moral sufferings, I am in no position to judge them, you will take a sounder view than I can –

> 'Nave nave mahana.' Delightful days.
> 'Bunch of flowers.'
> 'Note aha oe riri.' Why are you angry, girl?
> 'Barbaric poems.'
> 'Still-life.'
> 'Study after myself',

One of the pictures that Gauguin sent back from Tahiti in 1897 was 'Nave Nave Mahana' – Delightful Days.

just for something to paint – I offer it to you as a very paltry evidence
of friendship in return for all your affection. And if you particularly
like one of the pictures, take it: I should be very glad to give it to you.

I am trying to finish a picture so as to send it with the others, but *shall
I have time?* Be careful to keep it upright when you put it on the stretcher;

163

I don't know if I am mistaken, but I think it is good. I wanted, with a simple, naked figure, to suggest a certain old-time barbaric luxury. It is all bathed in colours that are deliberately dark and gloomy; the luxury is neither in silk nor velvet, cambric nor gold, but solely in the substance made rich by the artist's hand. No bunkum . . . man's imagination alone has enriched the dwelling by its fantasy.

For title, 'Never more'; not Edgar Poe's raven, but the devil's bird that is on the watch. It is badly painted (my nerves are on edge and I work in fits and starts), never mind, I think it's a good picture – A naval officer will send you the lot in a month, I hope.

PAUL GAUGUIN TO GEORGES DANIEL DE MONFREID

February 1898

I didn't write to you last month, I had nothing more to say to you except repetitions, and then I had not the heart. As soon as the mail arrived, having received nothing from Chaudet, my health all at once almost recovered, that is to say with no further chance of dying a natural death, I wanted to kill myself. I went off to hide in the mountains, where my corpse would have been devoured by the ants. I had no revolver, but I had some arsenic, treasured up during my attack of eczema; I don't know whether the dose was too strong or whether the vomiting cancelled the effect of the poison by throwing it up. Anyhow, after a night of terrible suffering, I went home. . . . This month I receive 700 fr. from Chaudet and 150 fr. from Mauffra: with that I shall pay the most relentless of my creditors and go on yet again, living as before, in poverty and disgrace until May, when the bank will distrain on me and sell for a song what little I possess, my pictures among the rest. Well, when that time comes we'll see how to try again in some other way. I may say that my mind was definitely made up for the month of December. So before dying I wanted to paint a large picture I had in my head, and right through the month I worked day and night in an extraordinary fever. Of course it's not done like a Puvis de Chavannes, with studies from nature, a preliminary cartoon, etc. It was all done without a model, dashed off, on a coarse knotty piece of sacking, so it looks terribly rough.

PAUL GAUGUIN TO GEORGES DANIEL DE MONFREID

La Dominique (Hiva-Oa), Marquesas Islands, November 1901

You know my views on all these erroneous views of symbolist or other literature with regard to painting; so there is no point in repeating them; besides we are agreed on the subject – so is posterity – for sound work survives all the same, and no amount of critico-literary lucubration makes any difference to it. I may perhaps be too arrogant in praising myself for not having fallen into all the failings into which a favourable press would have led me like so many others – Denis, for example; Redon too, perhaps. And I used to smile, although I was annoyed, when I read so many critics who did not understand me.

Anyhow, in my loneliness here I can gather new strength. Here poetry emanates from things of its own accord and one need only let oneself dream when painting to suggest it. – All I ask is two years' good health and not too many money worries, which now have an excessive hold on my nervous temperament, in order to arrive at a certain maturity in my art. I can feel that in art *I am right*, but shall I have the strength to express it positively! In any case I shall have done my duty, and even if my work does not survive, what will survive is the memory of an artist who liberated painting from many of its former academic failings and from symbolist failings (another kind of sentimentality).

My letter will arrive in time to bring you New Year wishes –

My book, *Noa-Noa*, has been printed *without my knowledge*. If you can lay hands on it, send me a copy.

Best wishes to my friends and Annette,

Ever cordially yours,
Paul Gauguin

Earlier in this year (1901) Gauguin had made his final move, leaving Tahiti for the Marquesas Islands, the outermost of the Pacific Islands. 'Noa-Noa' is a description of his first residence in Tahiti and of his love for the Polynesian girl Tehura.

PAUL GAUGUIN TO GEORGES DANIEL DE MONFREID

La Dominique (Hiva-Oa), Marquesas Islands, April 1903

My dear Daniel,

I am sending you 3 pictures which you will probably receive after your letter. Will you tell Mr Fayet that it is a question of rescuing me. If the pictures do not suit him, let him take others from your place, or lend me 1,500 fr. with whatever security he wants – This is why: I have just fallen into a terrible trap. – After scandalous happenings in the Marquesas, I had written to the Administration, asking them to investigate the matter. I had not reflected that the police all hang together, that the Administrator belongs to the Governor's party, etc., anyhow the lieutenant called for proceedings and a bandit of a judge, obeying the orders of the Governor and of the little procurator I had slated, has sentenced me (law of July '81 on the Press) for a private letter, to 3 months' imprisonment and a fine of 1,000 fr. – I have to go to Tahiti to appeal. The journey, the time there, and above all the *lawyer's fees*!! how much will all that cost me? It means my ruin and the complete break-up of my health.

All my life I seem doomed to fall, pick myself up, fall again, etc. . . . All my one-time energy is dwindling day by day –

So do act quickly and be sure to tell Mr Fayet that I shall be eternally grateful to him –

Ever cordially yours.

Paul Gauguin

Here is the mail: still nothing from you – Vollard has not written me for the last 3 times and sends me no money at all. At present he owes me 1,500 fr. plus a balance for the pictures I sent him. As a result, I owe 1,400 fr. to the Société Commerciale, just at the moment when I have to ask them again for money to go to Papeete, etc. . . I very much fear they will refuse, and then I shall be in terrible straits. If he were dead or bankrupt, I venture to hope you would have been told of it. All these worries *are killing me.*

P. Gauguin

Gauguin died a month after this letter was written, on 6 May 1903, in utter solitude, in the house that he had built for himself and decorated with the inscription 'Maison du Jouir'.

'. . . before dying I wanted to paint a large picture I had in my head' – *the picture was 'Where do we come from? What are we? Where are we going?' reproduced here in three parts. The sequence in the complete picture is from right to left. Below right:* 'a sleeping baby and three squatting women. . . . Two figures dressed in purple are exchanging their thoughts.' *Below left:* 'one figure . . . raises her arm and gazes in amazement at the two who dare to think about their future fate. A figure in the centre is picking a fruit.' *Right:* 'The idol, its arms raised mysteriously, gracefully, seems to be pointing to the beyond . . . last comes an old woman, near death.'

VINCENT VAN GOGH TO HIS BROTHER THEO

Laeken, 15 November 1878

I enclose that hasty little sketch, 'Au Charbonnage'. I should like to begin making rough sketches of some of the many things that I meet on my way, but as it would probably keep me from my real work, it is better not to start. As soon as I came home, I began a sermon about the barren fig tree, Luke 13: 6–9. The little drawing 'Au Charbonnage' is not particularly remarkable, but I made it because one sees here so many people who work in the coal mines, and they are a rather distinctive type. This little house stands not far from the road; it is a small inn which adjoins the big coal shed, and the workmen come to eat their bread and drink their glass of beer there during the lunch hour.

When I was in England, I applied for a position as evangelist among the coal miners, but they put me off, saying I had to be at least twenty-five years old. You know how one of the roots or foundations, not only of the Gospel, but of the whole Bible is 'Light that rises in the darkness', *from darkness to light.* Well, who needs this most, who will be receptive to it? Experience has shown that the people who walk in the darkness, in the centre of the earth, like the miners in the black coal mines, for instance, are very much impressed by the words of the Gospel, and believe them, too. Now in the south of Belgium, in Hainaut, near Mons, up to the French frontier – aye, even far across it – there is a district called the Borinage, which has a unique population of labourers who work in the numerous coal mines. . . .

If I could work quietly in such a district for about three years, always learning and observing, then I should not come back without having something to say that was really worth hearing. I say this in all humility and yet with confidence. If God wills, and if He spares my life, I would be ready by about my thirtieth year – beginning with my own unique training and experience, mastering my work better and being riper for it than now.

I am writing you this again, although we have already discussed it many a time.

There are many little Protestant communities in the Borinage already, and certainly schools, also. I wish I could get a position there as an evangelist in the way we talked about, preaching the Gospel to the poor – those who need it most and for whom it is so well suited – and then devoting myself to teaching during the week.

Vincent van Gogh (1853–1890) was the son of a Dutch pastor from whom he inherited a deeply religious nature. After working for the same firm of art-dealers as his brother Theo, in The Hague, Paris, and London, he taught in England for a while, and then began to study for the Church. In 1878 he became a lay preacher and went to work among the miners in the Borinage district of Belgium. Two years were to elapse before Van Gogh took up painting as a career. In the meantime he was already making sketches, many of which were drawn to illustrate points in his letters.

VINCENT VAN GOGH TO HIS BROTHER THEO
Nuenen, 30 April 1885

Dear Theo,

On your birthday I am sending you my best wishes for good health and serenity. I should have liked to send you the picture of the potato eaters on that day, but though it is getting on well, it is not quite finished yet.

Though the ultimate picture will have been painted in a relatively short time and for the greater part from memory, it has taken a whole winter of painting studies of heads and hands.

And as to those few days in which I have painted it now, it has been a real battle, but one for which I feel great enthusiasm. Although I was repeatedly afraid I should never pull it off. . . .

If you could compare the first painted studies I made on my arrival here at Nuenen and the picture I'm now working on, I think you would see that things are getting a little more lively as to colour. . . .

As to the potato eaters, it is a picture that will show well in gold, I am sure of that, but it would show as well on a wall, papered in the deep colour of ripe corn.

It simply cannot be seen without such a setting.

It does not show up well against a dark background, and not at all against a dull background. That's because it gives a glimpse of a very

'The Potato Eaters', which, wrote Van Gogh, needs 'a wall papered in the deep colour of ripe corn.'

grey interior. In reality too it stands in a gold frame, as it were, because the hearth and the glow of the fire on the white wall would be nearer to the spectator, now they are outside the picture, but in reality they throw the whole thing into perspective.

I repeat, it must be shut off by framing it in something of a deep gold or brass colour.

If you yourself want to see it as it must be seen, don't forget this, please. This putting it next to a gold tone gives, at the same time, a brightness *to spots where you would not expect it,* and takes away the marbled aspect

'Pavement Café at Night.' Van Gogh describes this painting in his letter of September 1888.

it gets when unfortunately placed against a dull or black background. The shadows are painted in blue, and a gold colour puts life into this. . . .

I have tried to emphasize that those people, eating their potatoes in the lamplight, have dug the earth with those very hands they put in the dish, and so it speaks of *manual labour*, and how they have honestly earned their food.

I have wanted to give the impression of a way of life quite different from that of us civilized people. Therefore I am not at all anxious for everyone to like it or to admire it at once.

All winter long I have had the threads of this tissue in my hands, and have searched for the ultimate pattern; and though it has become a tissue of rough, coarse aspect, nevertheless the threads have been chosen carefully and according to certain rules. And it might prove to be a real *peasant picture. I know it is.* But he who prefers to see the peasants in their Sunday-best may do as he likes. I personally am convinced I get better results by painting them in their roughness than by giving them a conventional charm.

I think a peasant girl is more beautiful than a lady, in her dusty, patched blue skirt and bodice, which get the most delicate hues from weather, wind and sun. But if she puts on a lady's dress, she loses her peculiar charm. A peasant is more real in his fustian clothes in the fields than when he goes to church on Sunday in a kind of dress coat.

In the same way it would be wrong, I think, to give a peasant picture a certain conventional smoothness. If a peasant picture smells of bacon, smoke, potato steam – all right, that's not unhealthy; if a stable smells of dung – all right, that belongs to a stable; if the field has an odour of ripe corn or potatoes or of guano or manure – that's healthy, especially for city people.

Such pictures may *teach* them something. But to be perfumed is not what a peasant picture needs.

Van Gogh is proclaiming his belief in unsentimental realism while painting his famous study of Flemish peasants at their supper, 'The Potato Eaters'. He had spent the previous winter preparing for this picture and had painted over fifty portraits of local peasants.

VINCENT VAN GOGH TO HIS SISTER WILLEMIEN

Arles, about 8 September 1888

My house here is painted the yellow colour of fresh butter on the out-side with glaringly green shutters; it stands in the full sunlight in a square which has a green garden with plane trees, oleanders and acacias. And it is completely whitewashed inside, and the floor is made of red bricks. And over it there is the intensely blue sky. In this I can live and breathe, meditate and paint. And it seems to me that I might go still farther into the South, rather than go up to the North again, seeing that I am greatly in need of a strong heat, so that my blood can circulate normally. Here I feel much better than I did in Paris.

You see, I can hardly doubt that you on your part would also like the South enormously. The fact is that the sun has never penetrated us people of the North. It is already a few days since I started writing this letter, and now I will continue it. In point of fact I was interrupted these days by my toiling on a new picture representing the outside of a night café. On the terrace there are the tiny figures of people drinking. An enormous yellow lantern sheds its light on the terrace, the house front and the side-walk, and even casts a certain brightness on the pavement of the street, which takes a pinkish violet tone. The gable-topped fronts of the houses in a street stretching away under a blue sky spangled with stars are dark blue or violet and there is a green tree. Here you have a night picture without any black in it, done with nothing but beautiful blue and violet and green, and in these surroundings the lighted square acquires a pale sulphur and greenish citron-yellow colour. It amuses me enormously to paint the night right on the spot. They used to draw and paint the picture in the daytime after the rough sketch. But I find satisfaction in painting things immediately.

In February 1888 Van Gogh had moved to the South of France. He settled in Arles and was later joined by Gauguin, with catastrophic results. Despite the fact that it was at Arles that Van Gogh fell victim to the mental illness that resulted in his suicide in 1890, he was delighted by the Midi. The dazzling sun-light and the harsh, bright colours inspired some of his finest paintings.

JAMES ENSOR ON HIS FIRST BRUSSELS EXHIBITION

The very first time I exhibited, at La Chrysalide, although my intentions were peaceful, I upset pictorial convention. The critics vied with each other in tearing me to pieces . . . I was abused, insulted, proclaimed a madman, a fool; I was called nasty, bad, incapable, and ignorant. A simple cabbage somehow became obscene; my placid interiors, my bourgeois salons, hotbeds of revolution . . . the critics multiplied their attacks, the most savage blows being exchanged with passion. For ten years they snarled without let-up, strangled without mercy.

James Ensor (1860–1949), the Belgian painter and engraver, was one of the most original and uncompromisingly unconventional artists to appear in Europe towards the end of the nineteenth century. He was born in Ostend, where he spent most of his long life, and showed talent at an early age. When he first exhibited his work at Brussels in 1881 with a group called 'La Chrysalide' the stormy reception accorded to it was the first of his many clashes with critical opinion throughout his long career.

'. . . here is vermilion! and cobalt blue! and lemon yellow!' *Ensor's* 'The Entry of Christ into Brussels' *owes some of its qualities to the fact that the artist (for financial reasons) used cans of modified house paint instead of oil pigment.*

JAMES ENSOR IN HIS 'REFLECTIONS ON ART'

1882

Our vision is modified as we observe. The first vision, that of the vulgar herd, is the simple line, unadorned, unconcerned with colour. The second stage is when the better-trained eye discerns values of the tones and their subtleties; this stage is less well understood by the vulgar herd. The last stage is when the artist sees the subtleties and multiple plays of light, its planes, its gravitations. These progressive explorations modify the original vision, and the line suffers and is relegated to a secondary role. This vision will be little comprehended. It requires long observation and attentive study. The vulgar herd sees in it only disorder, chaos and inaccuracy.

In this same year Ensor had two works exhibited at the Paris Salon, but it was not long before he was shocking his contemporaries, and arousing the violent hostility of critics by his grotesque imagery and unusual colouring. His largest, most famous and controversial painting was 'The Entry of Christ into Brussels'. Ensor was not shy about revealing his own feelings about his creation:

'I recorded her graceful features on a panel of good quality.' *Ensor's 'Consoling Virgin' combines Symbolism, a sort of Pre-Raphaelite simplicity and a highly individual confession of faith.*

JAMES ENSOR ON HIS PAINTING 'THE ENTRY OF CHRIST INTO BRUSSELS'

'The Entry of Christ into Brussels' . . . teems with the hard and soft creatures that the sea throws up . . . the irony and splendour of it all captivated and touched me, refining my vision. My colours are purified, they are integral and personal. . . . Ah, I said, you don't enjoy my motley masks! Well, then, here is vermilion! and cobalt blue! and lemon yellow! . . . You won't like it, but I'll give you pure tones!

Although it was painted in 1888 it was only in 1929 that it was publicly exhibited for the first time. The same year Ensor was made a baron by the King of Belgium.

JAMES ENSOR ON WORDS

Ah, but I love to draw beautiful words, like trumpets of light . . . I adore you, words who are sensitive to our sufferings, words in red and lemon yellow, words in the steel-blue colour of certain insects, words with the scent of vibrant silks, subtle words of fragrant roses and sea-weed, prickly words of sky-blue wasps, words with powerful snouts, words of spotless ermine, words spat out by the sands of the sea, words greener than the Cyrene fleece, discreet words whispered by fishes in the pink ears of shells, bitter words, words of fleur-de-lis and Flemish corn-flowers, sweet words with a pictorial ring, plaintive words of horses being beaten, evil words, festive words, tornado and storm-tossed words, windy words, reedy words, the wise words of children, rainy, tearful words, words without rhyme or reason, I love you! I love you!

Ensor's prose was as uninhibited as his painting: when he was not indulging in violent polemics, writing pamphlets, articles and introductions to catalogues of his exhibitions, he used words to express his visual experiences and innermost feelings with poetic verve and spontaneity. The above is a good example of his high-spirited, colourful style teeming with metaphors and almost surrealist imagery.

JAMES ENSOR DESCRIBES THE BEACH AT OSTEND

The beach is extraordinarily animated. It is a strangely mottled world. Swells in well-cut flannels rampant on a field of sand. Mussels heaped upon mussels. Attractive little pieces teasing soft crablike creatures. Slender Englishwomen stride angularly by. Bathers carrying their pachydermic shapes on broad flat feet. Toadlike peasant-women. Screeching females with broad bottoms. Rubes soaping their grimy feet. Grotesque gambollings. A rapacious tribe that sickens all sensitive souls and litters the lovely, delicately toned beach.

Ensor found engraving a perfect medium for expressing his sardonic outlook on society and he portrayed just such a scene in his engraving 'The Beach at Ostend' of 1899 which is, at the same time, a satire on the fashionable, sentimental type of genre painting that was then in vogue.

JAMES ENSOR ON HIS PAINTING THE 'CONSOLING VIRGIN'

I had a glimpse of the Consoling Virgin, and I recorded her graceful features on a panel of good quality. I was quite young then. I felt the material of her blond cloak, I kissed her little feet of snow and mother-of-pearl. On the hard substance of the old panel the diaphanous image can still be made out; I guard it jealously; it is mine, and I love it.

No painting reveals Ensor's passionate devotion to his art more than his 'Consoling Virgin' of 1892. Here he shows himself kneeling in humble adoration before his muse ready to receive her blessing. The work is conceived in the style of an Annunciation, in which the artist takes the part of the Virgin. It was this bold adaptation of conventional imagery that enraged so many of his critics and typifies his work.

177

PAUL CÉZANNE TO ÉMILE ZOLA

Aix-en-Provence, 14 April 1878

My dear Émile,

I am just back from Marseilles, that will explain my long delay in answering you. I could not get your letter until last Thursday. Thank you for what you sent, both times. I am writing under my father's eye.

Going to Marseilles, I had the company of Monsieur Gibert. Such people see clearly, but they have the teacher's eye. As the train was taking us past Alexis' place, a staggering subject for a picture came into view towards the east: Ste-Victoire and the crags above Beaurecueil. I said, 'What a splendid subject'; he replied, 'The lines are too symmetrical.' – Referring to *L'Assommoir*, about which, incidentally, he was

'The Card Players' – a subject that fascinated Cézanne. This version is in the Louvre. From an everyday theme he builds up a composition of classical dignity.

the first person to speak to me, he said some very sound things, and praised it, but always from the point of view of technique! Then, after a long interval, he went on again, 'One would need to have made very advanced studies – to have been through the École Normale.' I had mentioned Richepin to him; he said 'There's no future in that.' How illogical – that's a man who has been through it. – But at that he is undoubtedly the person most interested in art, and most knowledgeable about it, in a town of 20,000 souls.

– I shall be good, I shan't manage to be clever.

I wish you good health, present my respects to Madame Zola, and thank you.

Paul Cézanne

'. . . sensations of colour which produce light give rise to abstractions.' *Cézanne's 'Still-life with Onions and Bottle' can be analysed in both naturalistic and abstract terms.*

Paul Cézanne (1839–1906), a native of Aix-en-Provence, was the son of a banker who had intended him for the law. Here he is writing to Zola, who had been a friend since their boyhood together at Aix, after returning from Paris where he had been working for several years after overcoming his father's opposition. He had acquired a mistress who with their infant son, had come to live at Marseilles and as he was still living on an allowance from his father, from whom he was keeping his liaison a secret, he been obliged to ask Zola for loans in order to support his 'family'. This was a time of great strain for Cézanne for in addition to his financial worries he had failed to achieve any success in Paris and his works exhibited in the Impressionist Exhibition of the previous year had been savagely attacked by the critics. His mention of the Mont Ste-Victoire is interesting: this mountain was to inspire him throughout his life.

PAUL CÉZANNE TO ÉMILE BERNARD

Aix-en-Provence, 15 April 1904

Dear Monsieur Bernard,

By the time this letter reaches you, you will very probably have received one coming from Belgium, I think, and addressed to you via the Rue Boulegon. I am happy to have the evidence of warm sympathy in art which you so kindly give me in the form of your letter.

Allow me to repeat what I said when you were here: deal with nature by means of the cylinder, the sphere and the cone, all placed in perspective, so that each side of an object or a plane is directed towards a central point. Lines parallel to the horizon give breadth, a section of nature or, if you prefer, of the spectacle spread before our eyes by the *Pater Omnipotens Aeterne Deus*. Lines perpendicular to that horizon give depth. But for us men, nature has more depth than surface, hence the need to introduce in our vibrations of light, represented by reds and yellows, enough blue tints to give a feeling of air.

I would like to say that I have had another look at your study of the ground floor of the studio, it is good. All you need do, I think, is to continue along these lines, you have an understanding of what ought to be done, and you will soon be able to turn your back on the Gauguins and Van Goghs!

Please thank Mme Bernard for her kind remembrance of the under-signed, give the children a kiss from 'Père Goriot', and my best respects to your family.

Émile Bernard was a minor painter and an art critic who had met Cézanne for the first time earlier in this same year though he had written an article praising his work as early as 1890. Cézanne wrote him a number of letters in which he put forward some of his most strongly held views on painting. Cézanne's letters, though, are really a kind of thinking aloud. He would have no pupils and laid down no theories. However his remarks, usually torn from their context, have prompted a great many theoretical reflections and his injunction to 'deal with nature by means of the cylinder, the sphere and the cone' has become famous.

Émile Bernard, the recipient of Cézanne's famous letter about 'the cylinder, the sphere and the cone' was a painter preoccupied with the theory of art and a believer in the symbolic qualities of colour. This 'Still-life' by him dates from 1890.

In this 'View of Gardanne' Cézanne turns the house-shapes into a complex of interlocking planes.

'Château Noir', painted towards the end of Cézanne's long life.

PAUL CÉZANNE TO ÉMILE BERNARD

Aix-en-Provence, 23 December 1904

My dear Bernard,
I have received your good letter from Naples. I will not launch out into
aesthetic reflections with you. Yes, I approve of your admiration for the
doughtiest Venetian of them all; we extol Tintoretto. Your need to find
moral and intellectual support in works which will certainly never be
excelled, keeps you perpetually on the alert, on an unceasing quest for   183

the half-perceived methods that will surely bring you to a sense of your means of expression in contact with nature; and once you master those, you can be certain that you will rediscover, without effort and in contact with nature, the means employed by the four or five great Venetian painters.

This is what happens, unquestionably – I am positive: an optical sensation is produced in our visual organ, which leads us to classify as light, half-tone or quarter-tone, the planes represented by sensations of colour. (Thus, light does not exist for the painter.) As long as, inevitably, one proceeds from black to white, the former of these abstractions being a kind of point of rest both for eye and brain, we flounder about, we cannot achieve self-mastery, get possession of ourselves. During this period (I tend to repeat myself, inevitably) we turn to the admirable works handed down to us through the ages, in which we find comfort and support, like a plank to the swimmer. – Everything you say in your letter is quite true.

I am glad to hear that Madame Bernard, yourself and the children are all well. My wife and son are in Paris at the moment. We shall be together again soon, I trust.

I hope to answer the principal points in your good letter so far as possible. Please ask Madame Bernard to accept my respectful greetings and give Antoine and Irène a kiss from me. As for you, my dear *confrère*, I wish you a happy New Year, with a warm clasp of the hand.

P. Cézanne

PAUL CÉZANNE TO ÉMILE BERNARD

Aix-en-Provence, 23 October 1905

My dear Bernard,

I value your letters for two reasons, the first of which is entirely selfish since their arrival jerks me out of the monotony induced by the uninterrupted pursuit of my one and only aim, which, at moments of physical fatigue, brings on a sort of intellectual exhaustion, and the second is the opportunity they give me of harking back, rather too constantly no doubt, to an account of the obstinacy with which I pursue the attempt to render that part of nature which, when it comes before our eyes, presents us with a picture. The point to be made clear is that, whatever may be our temperament, or our power in the presence of nature, we have to render what we actually see, forgetting everything that appeared before our own time. Which, I think, should enable the artist to express his personality to the full, be it large or small.

Now that I am an old man, about seventy, the sensations of colour which produce light give rise to abstractions that prevent me from covering my canvas, and from trying to define the outlines of objects when their points of contact are tenuous and delicate; with the result that my image or picture is incomplete. For another thing, the planes become confused, superimposed; hence Neo-Impressionism, where everything is outlined in black, an error which must be uncompromisingly rejected. And nature, if consulted, shows us how to achieve this aim.

Indeed I remembered you were at Tonnerre, but owing to the difficulties I meet with in trying to settle down at home I have put myself entirely in the hands of my family, with the result that they arrange what suits themselves and tend to forget me. Such is life; at my age I should have more experience and make use of it for the good of all. I owe you the truth in painting, and I will give it to you.

Please give my respects to Madame Bernard; the children I am bound to be fond of, St Vincent de Paul being the one to whom I should most commend myself. Your old
Paul Cézanne

A warm hand-clasp, and push ahead.
The visual sense, as it develops in us by dint of study, teaches us to see.

In Cézanne's constant exhortations to keep 'in contact with nature' we see the influence of Pissarro who had taught him that only in contact with nature could the artist develop his personality to the full, and his ambition was to 'do Poussin over again, but in front of nature'. Cézanne was against all theories and was resolutely hostile to all official artistic activities, declaring that the artist's function was to give concrete form to his sensations and perceptions with pencil and brush.

JAMES MCNEILL WHISTLER TO 'THE WORLD'

London, 22 May 1878

Why should not I call my works 'symphonies', 'arrangements', 'harmonies', and 'nocturnes'? I know that many good people think my nomenclature funny and myself 'eccentric'. Yes, 'eccentric' is the adjective they find for me.

The vast majority of English folk cannot and will not consider a picture as a picture, apart from any story which it may be supposed to tell.

My picture of a 'Harmony in Grey and Gold' is an illustration of my meaning – a snow scene with a single black figure and a lighted tavern. I care nothing for the past, present, or future of the black figure, placed there because the black was wanted at that spot. All that I know is that my combination of grey and gold is the basis of the picture. Now this is precisely what my friends cannot grasp.

'*Old Battersea Bridge: Nocturne – blue and gold.*'

(*Opposite*) 'What can or ought the public to care about the identity of the portrait?' '*The Artist's Mother: Arrangement in grey and black.*'

They say, 'Why not call it "Trotty Veck", and sell it for a round harmony of golden guineas?' – naïvely acknowledging that, without baptism, there is no . . . market!

But even commercially this stocking of your shop with the goods of another would be indecent – custom alone has made it dignified. Not even the popularity of Dickens should be invoked to lend an adventitious aid to art of another kind from his. I should hold it a vulgar and meretricious trick to excite people about Trotty Veck when, if they really could care for pictorial art at all, they would know that the picture should have its own merit, and not depend upon dramatic, or legendary, or local interest.

As music is the poetry of sound, so is painting the poetry of sight, and the subject-matter has nothing to do with harmony of sound or of colour.

The great musicians knew this. Beethoven and the rest wrote music – simply music; symphony in this key, concerto or sonata in that.

On F or G they constructed celestial harmonies – as harmonies – as combinations, evolved from the chords of F or G and their minor correlatives.

This is pure music as distinguished from airs – commonplace and vulgar in themselves, but interesting from their associations, as, for instance, 'Yankee Doodle', or 'Partant pour la Syrie'.

Art should be independent of all clap-trap – should stand alone, and appeal to the artistic sense of eye or ear, without confounding this with emotions entirely foreign to it, as devotion, pity, love, patriotism, and the like. All these have no kind of concern with it; and that is why I insist on calling my works 'arrangements' and 'harmonies'.

Take the picture of my mother, exhibited at the Royal Academy as an 'Arrangement in Grey and Black'. Now that is what it is. To me it is interesting as a picture of my mother; but what can or ought the public to care about the identity of the portrait?

The imitator is a poor kind of creature. If the man who paints only the tree, or flower, or other surface he sees before him were an artist, the king of artists would be the photographer. It is for the artist to do something beyond this: in portrait painting to put on canvas something more than the face the model wears for that one day: to paint the man, in short, as well as his features; in arrangement of colours to treat a flower as his key, not as his model.

This is now understood indifferently well – at least by dressmakers. In every costume you see attention is paid to the key-note of colour which runs through the composition, as the chant of the Anabaptists through the *Prophète*, or the Hugenots' hymn in the opera of that name.

James McNeill Whistler (1834–1903) was born in Lowell, Massachussetts, and after attending West Point Military Academy and working as a navy cartographer, which taught him the technique of etching, he went to Paris at the age of twenty-one and studied painting. He lived in London from 1859 onwards. Whistler could express his aesthetic views with considerable vigour and wit, as this letter shows. In this same year he successfully sued John Ruskin for describing one of his 'Nocturnes' as 'flinging a pot of paint in the public's face'.

WALTER RICHARD SICKERT ON PAINTING AND CRITICISM
IN 'THE ART NEWS'

21 April 1910

Your correspondent raises questions I am only too ready to answer. I must begin with a protest – 'Cretin of a critic' is his phrase, and has never been mine. I must protest gently but firmly, against having expressions I have never used, quoted as from me. . . . Then I think it is a mistake to drag in snippets of foreign languages, that are not currently known in this country, into English prose compositions. I remember once how, wishing to give it immediate currency, I fathered a humble little *mot* of my own, in dog-Latin, on Whistler. With this sesame affiliation, my gem had the honours of immediate publication on the front page of the *Westminster Gazette*, under the line that separates the leader, on matters of importance, from the paragraphs of none. The next time I met Whistler he said: 'Very nice of you, very proper, to invent *mots* for me. "The Whistler *Mots* Propagation Bureau!" I know! Charming! Only when they are in languages I don't know, you had better advise me in good time, and send me a translation. Otherwise I am congratulated on them at dinner parties, and it is awkward.'

Now to the 'unlicensed valuer' theory of the art critic's function. Allow me to urge my constructive advice by a concrete instance. . . . My friend Cahen, the author of the book on Boudin we all know, bought Boudin's work over a period extending through the whole of the artist's life. Cahen is a lawyer. God has therefore given him a brain and eyes, three requisites for the carrying-on of even such a humble profession as the law. . . . Cahen seems to have suspected, arrogantly perhaps, that the above-mentioned organs were intended for use. It never for a moment occurred to him, that he had better nip round to the offices of the Paris newspapers and see what certain members of the respective staffs thought of Boudin.

> I want no stars
> In Heaven to guide me, etc.

This line of conduct has had its reward even here below. Works for which Cahen paid forty francs are now worth about £40, and works for which he paid £10 are worth anywhere between £200 and £400. When the time came, he sifted his collection, netted a small fortune from the annual investment he had made of a little pocket-money, and kept the pick of the work he loved for his own rooms. Is that or is that not a method of proceeding that recommends itself to the intelligence of a nation that is proud to be called a nation of shopkeepers?

Readers may have noticed that the sentimental stop in my organ is somewhat weak. Still I will point out, on the other side of the account, that Cahen, by his lifelong patronage, put an appreciable fraction of the necessary bread into the mouth of the fine painter that was Boudin. That he paid thus an appreciable fraction of Boudin's rent, and contributed largely, for his means, to the comfort and security of a great artist's production.

Now I will describe to you, briefly, the *modus operandi* of many a patron in this country.

Long, long after a painter's battle is lost or won, long after his stock has been safely housed in the dealer's cellars, our patron, being slightly deaf, and very slow-moving, and extremely suspicious, meets at dinner someone who tells him, what everyone has known for twenty years, that works signed with such-and-such names have gone up strangely in value.

'Dear me!' he says. 'You surprise me! Tut, tut, tut! I must see if I can't get some. What did you say was the name? Degas, Monet. Really?'

Scenting a profit, off he goes to the biggest dealers. 'I want to see some pictures by So-and-so, and So-and-so. What! Thousands of pounds? Impossible! Dear me! Well, let me have half a dozen at my house to look at for a while, so that I may choose at leisure.'

'Certainly, sir, if you will pay carriage and insurance.'

That is arranged to the satisfaction of both sides. Our patron then marches every expert he has ever met past this little 'appro' collection. Some of the experts are painters, some writers, some dealers, some ladies who have sat to a portrait-painter, and so rank as 'artistic'. One and all, having a sprat or two of their own to fry, crab the 'appro' collection,

Sickert was at one time a pupil of Whistler, and although his later style bears small trace of his master, he did resemble him in a certain cynicism, as his writings show. This self-portrait, painted when he was forty-eight, is called 'The Juvenile Lead'.

nicely, but unmistakably. Our patron, slightly discouraged, ends by picking out a very minor work by a name of the second rank, and pays a few hundreds for it. These hundreds include the original artist's price, interest on it for a matter of fifteen or twenty years, part rent of premises in Bond Street, or the Rue Laffitte for the same time, plus what the French call 'false expenses', postage, cabs, telegrams, and odds and ends of that kind. And note that patrons of this type consider themselves as real friends of the arts, that they generally frequent and prefer the society of artists, and are always slightly puzzled and aggrieved that they are not regarded with positive enthusiasm by the whole artistic profession.

Add to this that the purchase I have sketched above is a pure speculation. The patron has paid the full price of the name for a minor example. And we all know that, in any master's work, the tendency is for the masterpieces to go up, and the minor example down, with the sifting of time.

Walter Richard Sickert (1860–1942) was born in Munich, the son of a painter from Holstein who moved to London in 1868. He worked for a time in Whistler's London studio and met Degas in Dieppe, being greatly influenced by both artists. On his return to London he concentrated on paintings and drawings of music-hall, theatre and street scenes; and was also fascinated by the shabbiest parts of London such as Islington and Camden Town. Sickert was also an accomplished etcher. Unlike the Impressionists, with whom he has been compared, he vastly preferred painting urban scenes, particularly indoors, rather than landscapes. In 1911 he founded the Camden Town Group, later joining the London Group.

He was very much a man of the world and shared a good deal of Whistler's and Degas' dry wit and urbanity. He enjoyed writing and taking part in controversies, especially through the columns of newspapers and journals. The extract quoted above is a particularly good example of his lively style and his gift as a 'raconteur'.

Aubrey Beardsley – exquisite, sophisticated, neurotic, the epitome of fin-de-siècle decadence – is brilliantly caught in this portrait by Walter Sickert.

AUBREY BEARDSLEY TO LEONARD SMITHERS

Brussels, 3 May 1896

Dear Smithers many thanks for the 150 frs. I would have left to-morrow Raff^ch [André Raffalovich, a friend] pressed me to a lunch; & I should not have got any one to pack for me this evening as the whole hotel is occupied with the Grader marriage which has fluttered the bourgeoisie here tremendously. A perfectly gargantuan function. The hair was cut quite decently, my prayer was heard. Your continuation of the Limerick is superb & quite in the spirit of the first sublime couplet.

My blood by the way has long ceased to show the slightest inclination to spout. I have wired to my sister to pilot me over on Monday or to send somebody who is at liberty. At the last moment I funk the travelling; Dent's bill arrives to-morrow it cant be any thing very dreadful.

My work has been a little desultry but I have not been idle. My idea for the cover will be quite complete and matured when I have finished the drawing. The story of Hop on my thumb gets on. The Bacchanals have been spoilt, begun again & carried up to the point when the will alone is wanting. I drink uninteresting health to the Rape & Savoy at every meal.

Yours
A B

In the next room I hear laughter & a strange clapping of hands. Flemish lewdness is going forward, I doubt not, Belgian lubricity.

Aubrey Vincent Beardsley (1872–1898) left his stool in the counting-house of a London insurance company at the age of eighteen to devote himself to art. He was one of the most talented artists of the nineties, a leading figure in the new-style magazines—'The Yellow Book', 'The Studio' and 'The Savoy'. Oscar Wilde had just put fresh life into the epigram, and Beardsley drew epigrams in black and white, malicious, insolent, satirical commentaries on the books he illustrated. His drawings look as though they had been tossed off, but he was a meticulous worker, covering the paper with innumerable pencil strokes, erasing

Aubrey Beardsley: title-page for 'The Savoy' magazine and an illustration to Pope's 'The Rape of the Lock'

them and drawing over them until the whole sheet was one confused mass; then he drew his delicate, firm lines across the muddle, using Indian ink and a gold nib.

AUBREY BEARDSLEY TO LEONARD SMITHERS

Pier View, Boscombe
13 December 1896

My dear Smithers

How is Brussels? Yesterday I ventured out for a walklet in Winter gardens. As I was ascending the Chine blood began to spout profusely. Imagine my distress, with no possible way of getting home but on foot. I expected I should make an *al fresco* croak of it. I struggled *péniblement* to where I expected to find a drinking fountain. There *was* one there, & so the pretty creature drank. The cold water made things better, & I then

194

had the good luck to find a donkey chair to drag me the rest of the way to P.V. There seems to be no end to the chapter of blood.

I am better however, to-day.

How *is* Brussels?

Thanks for vol 3 of the Savoy.

Mother joins me in kindest regards to Mrs Smithers & yourself.

Yours
A B

So glad you will be able to spare time to come & see me miserable.

AUBREY BEARDSLEY TO LEONARD SMITHERS

Menton, 7 March 1898

Jesus is our Lord & Judge

Dear Friend

I implore you to destroy *all* copies of 'Lysistrata' & bad drawings. Show this to Pollitt & conjure him to do same. By all that is holy *all* obscene drawings.

Aubrey Beardsley
In my death agony

Nine days after writing this letter to Leonard Smithers, his publisher, Beardsley died of tuberculosis at the age of twenty-five—having already been a legendary figure for some four years. Smithers ignored his dying request to destroy his series of illustrations to Aristophanes' play 'Lysistrata' and they later appeared in a limited edition.

'The Herald.' One of the illustrations to 'Lysistrata' which Beardsley asked should be destroyed after his death.

HENRY VAN DE VELDE TO KARL SCHEFFLER

March 1899

Of all the studies of my work that have appeared up to now, yours is certainly the best . . .

Regarding myself, it had never yet been said 'that my art had a traditional basis'.

I have a deep and manifold sense of connection with the past, but it does not shackle me or prevent me from seeing ahead. So to that extent there is something a little different about me, don't you agree?

Another time you might go further and say that my art is classic too, for so it is, or at least tries to be. But don't let anyone criticize it as being academic. For the public takes those two terms to be synonymous. And what a silly idea! Don't our railway engines, in their functional beauty, our steamships, our covered markets and our iron bridges link us with the classical works, and aren't our engineers the direct descendants of the great architects? The latter have been driven from their command of tradition and the former have taken over the guardianship of the classical tradition.

Certainly I am related to Gothic art – through the spirit – but to early Gothic, Romanesque. In the later Gothic I find there is far too much of the fantastic – I have said somewhere else that I look on it as a burden to the spirit.

Your observation that Baroque and Rococo are not an end but a beginning, also reveals true critical profundity. But that point needs to be discussed further, like the relationship you think you can see between my work and that of those periods. I cannot go into the matter today, but I hope to write about it later on and clarify it for myself and others.

I shall soon come to terms with you on the subject, because you do not confuse the meaning and spirit of my decorative work with those of earlier periods; for they really are modern. I have already explained (article in *Pan*) why I set so little store by having revived the tradition of functional construction, even though that tradition may have led me to discover new and unknown forms. I prefer to think of myself as the creator of a new decorative art which is both intellectual and plastic.

A tapestry, 'Angels keeping Watch', by Henry van de Velde. The flowing lines of 'Art nouveau' are here used with an economy and strength that point beyond its date of 1891.

Henry van de Velde (1863–1957), the Belgian architect and designer, was one of the originators of the 'Art noveau' movement, or 'Jugendstil' as it was known in Germany where he worked for many years, and had taken part in the Dresden exhibition of 1897. He was strongly influenced by the ideas of Ruskin and Morris in England, particularly in their relation to arts and crafts. He was an active teacher and author, and a pioneer in the design of modern houses and theatres. His stimulating influence on younger artists and designers played a large part in determining the new stylistic trends that emerged in Europe in the early part of this century, and he was a forerunner of the 'Bauhaus' movement in Germany. In 1926 he settled in Brussels and founded an Institute of Decorative Art.

ANDRÉ DERAIN TO MAURICE VLAMINCK

1909

Maurice, old man,

I'm all alone here. From the social point of view I'm bored. But I'm doing an enormous amount of thinking. For instance I've had a new idea for a semi-symbolic play, with masks and music *ad hoc*. Quite stunning. I think it would be wonderfully dramatic.

I'm making a lot of little notes that you'll find useful. It's a pity you can't come here, just for a week. These 'landscape' landscapes are stunning and would please you tremendously. The atmosphere is delicate, delicate and colourful! . . .

All the same I'm going to do some landscapes, but grudgingly almost. I don't feel the need for landscapes, or for portraits or for still-lifes. I have had stunning sensations, the grandeur of which can find no equivalent except in an absolute mastery of the forms of which I make use indiscriminately, to convey it. It is difficult to achieve complete mastery of a landscape.

But it's easier to create a plastic harmony that one draws up from the depths of oneself, with the affection one bears to things in the physical universe.

Delacroix was quite right in saying that 'Nature is a dictionary; one draws words from it.' But above and beyond the dictionary there is the determination to write, the unity of our own thoughts; and that is merely the translation into space of our virility, our cowardice, our sensibility and our intelligence. All this, amalgamated, makes up the personality that expresses itself in plastic form.

For instance, the picture I sent to the 'Indépendants', the one with the three women, did it need to be better than it was? No! It could have given much more evidence of absolute determination without conveying any greater sense of a choice of direction.

I think we go wrong if we try to show only our virtues. The display of our defects and our blind spots is a definite affirmation that virtue is present in the next man, in an absolute sense. Thus, if my picture is not what it should have been, it is nevertheless sufficiently so to make it clear that someone else can bring it off! That's already something!

. . . You're no good except as a decorator! All right, that's perfectly true. But my intelligence and my will create a reality for themselves, by showing that they want to *go beyond the talents that fell to my lot.*

If I don't create an absolute for myself, I do at least render the equivalent of what I understand and of what I want.

I could write to you at great length on the subject; but it doesn't particularly interest me. What does interest me, and what I would like to talk to you about, is the modern outlook on life. I'm thinking about it intensely here. And it seems to me that everything conspires (or combines?) in the search for happiness. Now one cannot detach oneself completely, live superior to pleasure and pain; it does happen sometimes in intense artistic excitement. But when one comes down again, one gets it even worse. The maximum of joy is balanced by the maximum of bother.

Only one thing can save painting, and that is joking. Joking gets you out of anything. Joking is all-powerful. With a joke you can get yourself out of anything. Fundamentally, one is often very bothered; but one manages to adopt the spirit of the mask one puts on. That's what's so stunning about it. The thing is . . . to joke about something out of vexation . . . afterwards, you joke about your own mind.

Portrait of André Derain executed by Henri Matisse in the summer of 1905 when the two artists were painting their first 'Fauve' pictures.

On the other hand, greatness, enormousness, is a very stupid thing. What's a thing that's lofty, noble in sentiment, full of enthusiasm? If it sets out to be that, it's idiotic.

We are too uncertain of the trend of present-day ideas to aim at a definite character. We have to submit ourselves to the unconscious. As for the result, we cannot be the adepts of our own teaching.

In the same way, it is ridiculous to want to adopt an attitude; one must follow life's lead, voluntarily, extracting the maximum enjoyment from one's surroundings. When I say 'enjoyment' I don't mean one has to be physically happy. I am referring, above all, to the appraisal of this enjoyment.

My amorous adventure follows its course. Madame is plunged in the greatest difficulties. I don't know what she can be doing in Paris. I believe she is very worried. Otherwise I have no precise idea of what she can be thinking. The situation remains exactly the same. We write to each other and neither will give way. It gets more and more stunning. Write to me, for I'm so bored, all by myself.

Greetings.   A. Derain

If you could see her, you might sound her thoroughly; for as far as I'm concerned, I'm completely at a loss now.

André Derain (1880–1954) studied painting in Paris where he met and became friendly with Vlaminck and Matisse. He exhibited with them in 1905 at the Autumn Salon as a member of the group known as the 'Fauves' (Wild Beasts) for their use of violent colours and distorted forms. Derain worked in very close collaboration with Vlaminck for a while at Chatou. After the 'Fauves' broke up and he had disagreed with Vlaminck's art theories Derain went to Paris, becoming influenced by various other art schools and meeting Braque and Picasso during their 'Cubist' period. After the First World War Derain reverted to a much more traditional style of painting, using more sober colour. He also designed costumes and scenery for the ballet, in particular for Diaghilev's Russian company which visited Paris in 1919, and illustrated many books.

Despite his disagreements with Vlaminck, Derain remained on friendly terms and the two artists kept up a correspondence until the end of the First World War.

THE TWENTIETH CENTURY

'A largely unconscious, spontaneous expression of inner character, of non-material (i.e. spiritual) nature. This I call an *Improvisation*' – *Kandinsky in his treatise 'Das Geistige in der Kunst'*.

VASSILI KANDINSKY IN THE CATALOGUE OF THE SECOND
EXHIBITION HELD BY THE 'NEUE KÜNSTLERVEREINIGUNG'

Murnau, August 1910

The work comes into the world at an undetermined hour, from a source still unknown, but it comes inevitably.

Cold calculation, random spots of colour, mathematically exact construction (clearly shown or concealed), drawing that is now silent and now strident, painstaking thoroughness, colours like a flourish of trumpets or a pianissimo on the violin, great, calm, oscillating, splintered surfaces.

A detail from 'First Abstract' – a watercolour dating from the period of the 1910 Exhibition.

KANDINSKY 1910

Is this not form?

Is this not *the means*?

Suffering, searching, tormented souls, deeply sundered by the conflict between spirit and matter. Discovery! The part that is living in both animate and inanimate nature. Solace in the phenomena – the outer, the inner. Anticipation of joy. The call. To speak of mystery in terms of mystery.

Is this not content?

Is this not the conscious and unconscious *goal* of the compelling urge to create?

We feel sorry for those who have the power to speak for art, and do not.

We feel sorry for those whose souls are deaf to the voice of art.

Man speaks to man of the superhuman – the *language* of art.

Vassili Kandinsky (1866–1944) is regarded today as one of the chief founders of purely 'abstract' painting. He was born in Moscow where he studied law but later abandoned a legal career to travel extensively and take up painting in Munich, from 1896 onwards. In 1909 he became the president of an avant-garde group, the 'Neue Künstlervereinigung' (New Artists' Association), which gave two exhibitions in Munich. The second, which outraged the local press and public, was held in the same year in which Kandinsky painted his first 'abstract' picture and wrote his treatise on non-objective art, 'Uber das Geistige in der Kunst' (Concerning the Spiritual in Art), which was published in January 1912. The ideas he expresses in the preface to the catalogue of the second Munich exhibition are basically the same as those in his book. He wanted to show that form and colour alone could be used to express the inner emotion of the artist, and be combined into a new 'language' through which ideas could be communicated to the observer.

One of the woodcuts illustrating 'Uber das Geistige in der Kunst' which Kandinsky published in 1912.

Self-portrait by Paul Klee – a woodcut of 1911, the year of the first 'Blaue Reiter' exhibition.

PAUL KLEE TO 'DIE ALPEN'

Munich, 1912

Among the private galleries, the Thannhauser has again attracted my attention, with the (third) exhibition of the new association and its even more radical splinter group, known as the 'Blaue Reiter'. Keeping to the main idea, and ignoring extraneous developments and the many works which give a false impression of belonging to this movement, I would like to reassure people who cannot manage to trace it back to any of their favourites, even to El Greco. There is still an occasional artistic move-ment whose inception can be traced rather to some ethnographical collection, or to the nursery at home. Don't laugh, reader! Children have their own possibilities too, and that makes sense! The more innocent they are, the more instructive are the examples they set before us, and they too have to be sheltered at an early age from becoming corrupted. The work of lunatics is a parallel phenomenon; so that when people speak in this connection of childish behaviour or of madness, the words are not to be taken in the caustic spirit in which they are meant. All this is to be regarded with the greatest seriousness, more seriously than all the art galleries, if art is now to be reformed. If it is true, as I believe, that all the trends of the recent past are sinking into oblivion and that what are

'. . . I must begin, not with hypotheses, but with specific instances, no matter how minute', *wrote Klee in 1902, a phrase which shows how opposite his temperament was from Kandinsky's. 'Girl with Jugs' was painted in 1910.*

known as the undeviating followers of tradition have only an outward appearance of glowing health but are seen in the light of serious history as the embodiment of lassitude, then a great moment has arrived and I greet those who are contributing to the approaching reformation.

The boldest of those shown here is Kandinsky, who also tries to make his effects in words (*Das Geistige in der Kunst*, published by Piper).

Paul Klee (1879–1940), the son of a German father and Swiss mother, was born in Switzerland and studied painting at the Munich Academy of Art. He became friendly with Kandinsky, Franz Marc and August Macke and together they formed the avant-garde 'Blaue Reiter' (Blue Rider) group. Their first exhibition was held in 1911 at the Thannhauser gallery in Munich, and it included some of Klee's drawings. Klee wrote a great deal and from an early age he noted down his views and reflections on art. He was also a fine musician. The letter reproduced was written at a time when he was regularly contributing articles on the artistic and musical events in Munich to the Swiss review 'Die Alpen'.

FRANZ MARC TO THE PUBLISHER REINHARD PIPER

1908

I am trying to heighten my feeling for the organic rhythm in all things, trying to establish a pantheistic contact with the tremor and flow of blood in nature, in animals, in the air – trying to make it all into a picture, with new movements and with colours that reduce our old easel paintings to absurdity.

FRANZ MARC IN HIS MANIFESTO FOR THE 'BLAUE REITER' GROUP

1912

Art today is moving in directions of which our forebears had no inkling; the Horsemen of the Apocalypse are heard galloping through the air; artistic excitement can be felt all over Europe – new artists are signalling to one another from all sides; a glance, a touch of the hand, is enough to convey understanding . . .

Franz Marc's 'Yellow Horses', painted in 1912, is one of several variants on the same theme.

Franz Marc (1880–1916, killed at Verdun) was a Munich painter who in 1911 became, with Kandinsky, a leader of the 'Blaue Reiter' group. He preferred painting animals to human beings, whom he found ugly, declaring that they seemed 'purer and more beautiful' to him, and several of his animal studies were published in postcard form by the leading avant-garde magazine 'Der Sturm'.

FRANZ MARC TO HIS WIFE FROM THE FRONT, FIRST WORLD WAR

The Western Front, 17 April 1915

L . . . Koehler wrote to me today on his '*Sturm*' postcard of my '*Tierschicksale*'. I was quite astounded and agitated at the sight of it. It is like a presentiment of the war, terrible and gripping; I can hardly realize that I painted it myself! In the hazy photograph, at any rate, it has an indefinable reality that quite made my flesh creep. It is artistically logical to paint such pictures *before* a war, not as stupid reminiscences *after* a war. For one should paint constructive, prophetic pictures, not souvenirs, as is the usual fashion. And those are all I have in mind. It used to puzzle me sometimes, but now I know why it has to be like that. But these old pictures from the autumn Salon are sure to be resurrected again . . .

'It is like a presentiment of the war, terrible and gripping' – '*The Fate of Animals*' was painted in 1913, the year before the outbreak of the First World War. Marc had inscribed on the back, 'And all being is flaming suffering.'

ERNST BARLACH TO THE PUBLISHER REINHARD PIPER

31 December 1911

I have not yet settled down to *reading* Kandinsky's essay *Concerning the Spiritual in Art* properly, but I can see already that I shall be in no hurry to do so. Not that, from what I have caught in passing, I feel entitled, or even wish, to deny that the author has a penetrating intellect, on the contrary, but the book seems to be by no means what is called 'well-meant'. But this only brings a sharper click of the catch that reacts, or functions, in me; in other words I refuse to go along, instinctively. There is a yawning gulf that couldn't be deeper. Just lately I have often been obliged to assure people in various directions that I am simply a barbarian. And as a barbarian I am ready to believe the man when he declares sincerely that he gets a deep spiritual emotion (i.e. something more than the response of taste confronted with the ornamental) out of dots, flecks, lines and spots; but I can only take his word for it. And so goodbye! We could discuss it for a thousand years without coming to an understanding. After all, I am not without experience myself, I have been through periods when I sat and sat and 'created' lines. Those were the intervals, the pauses, when brain and hand were ready all right, but everything else seemed to have lost its cunning. Here I would like to use a word that you, as an admirer of Schopenhauer, will not think trivial: compassion. I must be able to feel compassion – if only with myself, if no other is possible – with myself for being so unworthy, so utterly unlike those who may well feel compassion for *me*. Compassion need not be doleful. I can sense it, too, in enjoyment of the heroic or the humorous. Or I might call it vicarious suffering or vicarious pleasure – on my part that is to say. A sympathy which carries understanding so far that it puts itself in the place of what it sees. Could you feel compassion for the forms shown on page 98, or would you care to be in the place of page 88. That's a question without a question-mark. Of course I could set my imagination to work on it, and make something out of it. I even believe most things, and the best of them, come into existence like that, that the effects of chance or the natural laws of chaos incite a disposition to use art as a means of forcing the virginity of what is untouched and indistinct, fertilizing it spiritually and rendering it communicable and consciously animated. Which would be just the opposite.

But we have to agree on a language, if we are to get to know anything at all: a man might tell me the most beautiful, magnificent things in Chinese and I shouldn't prick up my ears. So if I am to enter into a spiritual experience, it must be expressed in a language in which I can share the deepest and most secret experiences. My native tongue is the most suitable and in art my native tongue happens to be the human form or the milieu, the object through or within which the human being lives, suffers, rejoices, feels and thinks. I can't get beyond that. Nor can I accept an Esperanto art. It is precisely the touch of vulgarity, the universally human, the primitive sense of race, that are great and eternal. What man has suffered and can suffer, his greatness and his various concerns (including myths and dreams of the future) are what I am committed to, but my little personal feelings or my most individual sensations are irrelevant, nothing but moods, if they lead me out of the circle of humanity. Man as an ego must have his egotistical interest aroused, his higher and lower aspects or however you like to put it; but page 88 and page 98 don't stir my egoism in the least. Nor do I believe that a new artistic trend can be described *logically*, as Mr Kandinsky supposes – except as literature, as an intellectual achievement. But my criticism is worthless, for I, the author of it, am not of the same species as the writer and I can quite imagine a writer remaining unmoved by things that stir me to my very depths. He might say to me 'You are no artist, you're an actor! You "make believe" that certain feelings exist, whereas I generate ideas and feelings, moods and sensations as though by wireless telegraph – without an intervening medium, through direct transmission.' That would be all very well if feelings could be produced by agreement. One can easily say 'blue signifies this, yellow that'; but it is doubtful whether he has the divine power to set up his intentions as a standard. But when colour and line are created from human figures – or vice versa – they have power, for they derive it from the human soul. How often one sees colours and shapes on walls or in furniture which are suddenly transformed into a picture by imagination and the addition of something that animates them. Then it is drawn into my human

egoism; before that, it was something external. At most, the eternally hungry optic nerve may have been stimulated by it, because it was less boring, more colourful and charming than the rest of the surroundings. Human egoism can become interesting in ways quite unconnected with art, but that is another matter. Whether you will agree with what I say here, or whether you can make head or tail of it, is also a different matter . . .

Ernst Barlach (1870–1938), the German sculptor and graphic artist, played an important part in the Expressionist movement. He had been greatly influenced by a visit he had made to Russia in 1906 and this had inspired many of his finest wood-carvings, particularly his powerful studies of beggars and peasants. In his search for a style in which he could best communicate his feelings he returned to the forms of medieval German art and some of his finest work was intended for the Church. Like many other Expressionists he did woodcuts and lithographs in addition to his main work as a sculptor, and wrote plays and poems which he illustrated himself. Together with Klee and Kandinsky, among others, his work was to be anathema to the Nazis when they came to power and much of it was confiscated or destroyed.

'I must be able to feel compassion . . .'. 'Veiled Beggar Woman' – a wood-carving that looks back to fifteenth-century German and Burgundian sculpture.

MAX BECKMANN FROM THE FRONT, FIRST WORLD WAR

11 May 1915

I have such a passion for painting! I am continually working at form. In actual drawing, and in my head, and during my sleep. Sometimes I think I shall go mad, this painful, sensual pleasures tires and torments me so much. Everything else vanishes, time and space, and I think of nothing but how to paint the head of the resurrected Christ against the red constellations in the sky of Judgment Day . . . Or, how shall I paint Minkchen now, with her knees drawn up and her head leaning on her hand, against the yellow wall with her rose, or the sparkling light in the dazzling whiteness of the anti-aircraft shell-bursts in the leaden, sun-drenched sky and the wet, clear-cut, pointed shadows of the houses, or, or – I could write four pages like this if it were not time to go to sleep if I'm ever to paint even the hundredth part of it all.

MAX BECKMANN FROM THE FRONT, FIRST WORLD WAR

21 May 1915

The trenches wound in meandering lines and white faces peered from dark dug-outs – a lot of men were still preparing the positions, and everywhere among them there were graves. Where they sat, beside their dug-outs, even between the sandbags, crosses stuck out. Corpses jammed in among them. It sounds like fiction – one man was frying potatoes on a grave next to his dug-out.

The existence of life here had really become a paradoxical joke.

For that matter it's by no means certian that it is not one in fact, when we think of the circle of flame that blazes round us. In point of fact even that is not needed. When my mother died the world seemed just the same to me as it does now. The mystery of corpses pervading every-thing . . .

Minkchen was Beckmann's wife, Minna, for whom he signed nearly all his pictures from the First World War with 'MBSL' – 'Max Beckmann Seiner Lieben' (Max Beckmann to his love). She later published his wartime letters. Max Beckmann (1884–1950), the German painter and graphic artist received

'Self-portrait as a Medical Orderly.' Beckmann enlisted as a medical orderly on the outbreak of the First World War but had to be invalided out of the army the following year.

his first decisive impressions during the First World War. His early work made use of sharply contrasting black and white and included vigorous portraits and terse, bleak dry-point etchings. Later he turned to classical mythology, using rich colour to render its themes, but bringing to them the same basically tragic approach.

MAX BECKMANN IN HIS LECTURE 'DREI BRIEFE AN EINE MALERIN'

New York and Boston, Spring, 1948

Learn by heart the forms to be found in nature, so that you can use them like the notes in a musical composition. That is what these forms are for. Nature is a marvellous chaos, and it is our job and our duty to bring order into that chaos and – to perfect it. Leave it to others, to the colour-blind, to puzzle over old books on geometry or the problems of higher mathematics. We are going to enjoy the forms we see before our eyes.

A human face, a hand, a woman's breast or a manly body, an expression of conflicting joy and pain, the infinite ocean, savage crags, the melancholy speech of black trees against the snow, the fierce power of spring blossoms and the heavy lethargy of a hot summer noon when our old friend Pan is asleep and the ghosts of noon are murmuring – all this is enough to make us forget the sorrows of the world, or to give them form. In any case the determination to give form to things brings with it part of the solution for which you are seeking. The path is hard and the goal can never be reached – but it is a path.

'. . . how shall I paint Minkchen now, with . . . her head leaning on her hand', *wrote Beckmann from the Front in 1915. This portrait of his wife in a characteristic pose dates from 1930.*

PAUL NASH TO HIS WIFE

February 1917

The other night we had a most boring evening in the trenches and I wrote a certain amount to you by moonlight but have mislaid it, so here goes again. We entered the Seine early in the morning and began to move up slowly between its banks, at that time half-hidden in mists. As they cleared, the most enchanting country appeared. At the edge there were lines of poplars behind which stood ancient orchards, through the middle of which there ran a rough track or road up to the door of an old farm; such a place to live in, low and small with a conical shaped thatched roof and odd little casements, gables and dormer windows. Behind the farm there seemed a misty world of some sort, then cliffs, generally chalk, with caves in them and overhanging tufts of bushes. Sometimes we passed wide open country of hills, and saw the plough with the horses moving on a distant ridge. Other buildings were amusing little villas or still quiet white country houses with terraces. Once we passed a ferry where a peasant girl gave a ring to the bell to call the ferry. One of the men on board called out 'Ring ze bell again' which was received with howls and shouts of laughter. Some way up we passed a village, a gem of a place, where the church stood back only a short way from the water, with trees on either side of a rough road which sank into a ford in the winter. (This is probably Jumièges Abbey.) I was enchanted by it all and would have given much to have been dropped on one of these banks with leave to wander as long as I liked. At last the town was reached and I enjoyed my first meal in France. In the afternoon I visited the base depot where I met Coleman who made tender enquiries after you.

7 March 1917

They stopped post a day before we left, and it was impossible to write again till we got back to our old haunts. We are all sad to leave the quiet of that untroubled country, where such pleasant days have been spent. We could not have hit upon a better time for we saw all the change of trees and fields and hills from bleakness to fresh green and warm lovely lights. I must return to these landscapes above the hills. Just before I left I came upon a bank where real French violets grew, you know those dark ones that have such an intoxicating smell. Alas I was with the Company at the time, and though I meant to hunt out the bank after and send some flowers to you I never had time. Flowers bloom everywhere and we have just come up to the trenches for a time and where I sit now in the reserve line the place is just joyous, the dandelions are bright gold over the parapet and nearby a lilac bush is breaking into bloom; in a wood passed through on our way up, a place with an evil name, pitted and pocked with shells the trees torn to shreds, often reeking with poison gas – a most desolate ruinous place two months back, to-day it was a vivid green; the most broken trees even had sprouted somewhere and in the midst, from the depth of the wood's bruised heart poured out the throbbing song of a nightingale. Ridiculous mad in-congruity! One can't think which is the more absurd, the War or Nature; the former has become a habit so confirmed, inevitable, it has its grip on the world just as surely as spring or summer. Thus we poor beings are double enthralled. At the mercy of the old elements which we take pains to study, avoid, build and dress for we are now in the power of something far more pitiless, cruel and malignant, and so we must study further, build ten times as strong, dress cunningly and creep about like rats always overshadowed by this new terror. Of course we shall get used to it just as we are almost accustomed to the damnable climate of England. Already man has assumed an indifference quite extraordinary to shells, fire, mines and other horrors. It's just as well because it is going to be our daily bread for months and months to come.

I am rather pleased with myself just to-day because yesterday I sent off six finished sketches to you which after much labour I have managed to work up to a pitch of presentability. The C.O. has seen them and enclosed a note saying they are of no military importance and, as they are marked 'drawings' on the outside and registered and stamped by the field censor, I shouldn't wonder if they arrived unmolested. If they do, herewith a detail of orders for their disposition. They are numbered from 1 to 6 but my servant, usually intelligent, stupidly packed my notes about them, so I must describe them as best I can.

No. 1, as far as I can remember, was of trenches under a bloody sort of sunset with a crescent moon sailing above, to be called 'Winter Trenches'.

No. 2 is a rugged looking landscape with a scarred hill in the background and stick-like trees. The title 'Desolate Landscape'.

No. 3 of a ruined church – title 'Ruined Church, Belgium'.

No. 4 – Trenches in a wood – title 'Front Line Trench'.

No. 5 – French landscape, mostly sandbags, and a sky with a few stumps of trees and a moon – title 'French Landscape, St Eloi'.

No. 6 – A pool under evening sky – title 'The Pool'.

If you prefer to keep this last one for yourself, I have always thought of it as one for you if you would like to have it. When the drawings are mounted and framed they should go to Goupil, I am writing to Marchant about them. I will also write to Rowley. In a month or less I shall have another batch for you. Here in the back garden of the trenches it is amazingly beautiful – the mud is dried to a pinky colour and upon the parapet, and through sandbags even, the green grass pushes up and waves in the breeze, while clots of bright dandelions, clover, thistles and twenty other plants flourish luxuriantly, brilliant growths of bright green against the pink earth. Nearly all the better trees have come out, and the birds sing all day in spite of shells and shrapnel. I have made three more drawings all of these wonderful ruinous forms which excite me so much here. We are just by a tumbledown village, only heaps of bricks, toast-rackety roofs and halves of houses here and there among the bright trees and what remains of the orchards. This dug-out I am writing in must stand in what was once a snug cottage garden in hillocky ground sloping down to the stream, the apple trees fat with bloom straggle about outside the door, one has been knocked by a shell but continues flowering on its head. A green garden gate swung off its fence, leans up against the sandbags. I think it is the only significant landmark left. Our table inside is gay with a bunch of flowers – lilac, globe flowers, white narcissi found blooming near my trench, which is adjacent to the old village cottage gardens half a mile away. This place is the Mess, where I spend most of the time, though my actual responsibilities lie in 'M' trench which is held by my platoon. I feel very happy these days, in fact, I believe I am happier in the trenches than anywhere out here. It sounds absurd, but life has a greater meaning here and a new zest, and beauty is more poignant. I never feel dull or careless, always alive to the significance of nature who, under these conditions, is full of surprises for me. I can't quite explain my state of mind, not having troubled to analyse my emotions about it. Last night there was a heavy shelling, in fact the line is not the place it was; the Boche is very restive and jumpy, and I am not surprised. The clouds roll up in these parts and their shadows already fall over us. I have no fear. I know there are numerous things I want to say to you, but my mind is wandering to-day – it's raining and the earth and trees and all green things exude a moist perfume and make the soul dream wearily. . . . In the *New Statesman* you sent me, there is a short notice upon Edward Thomas saying the best thing he did was the verse written while he was in the Artists. He wrote under the name of Edward Eastaway. If you can procure any of his poems, I should so much like to read them. Some of my surplus kit has been sent home and soon I am going to post back all my books and get you to send me a few new ones which I will mention later. I read very little now, as a matter of fact between my drawing and writing letters my spare hours are pretty full.

'I have seen the most frightful nightmare of a country more conceived by Dante or Poe than by nature, unspeakable, utterly indescribable.' '*Mont St Eloi.*'

PAUL NASH TO HIS WIFE

16 November 1917

I have had to postpone this letter, it is even more difficult than it was when I was out last. I start off directly after breakfast and do not get home till dinner-time, and after that I work on my drawings until about 11 o'clock at night, when I feel very sleepy and go to bed. To-day, Sunday, has been more or less a holiday, so I motored down to take the old man out. We spent a great day and I have just got back (9 p.m.). The pre-vailing idea that he is depressed and hopeless is entirely wrong, he says he has never been so, and he seems to have got an enormous lot out of life over here. He is a real good soldier and very proud of it. Of course, he is dying to get home for a bit, and very keen now on getting a com-mission and wearing decent clothes again, but I assure you he has borne all the rough times magnificently, and he has really had it very rough. He is simply splendid and never stops talking of the good friends he has made and how they make the best of things and stick it out together. The whole thing has done him the world of good and as for wit it sparkles brighter than ever. . . . I have just returned, last night, from a visit to Brigade Headquarters up the line, and I shall not forget it as long as I live. I have seen the most frightful nightmare of a country more conceived by Dante or Poe than by nature, unspeakable, utterly indescribable. In the fifteen drawings I have made I may give you some vague idea of its horror, but only being in it and of it can ever make you sensible of its dreadful nature and of what our men in France have to face. We all have a vague notion of the terrors of a battle, and can conjure up with the aid of some of the more inspired war correspondents and the pictures in the *Daily Mirror* some vision of a battlefield; but no pen or drawing can convey this country – the normal setting of the battles taking place day and night, month after month. Evil and the incarnate fiend alone can be master of this war, and no glimmer of God's hand is seen anywhere. Sunset and sunrise are blasphemous, they are mockeries to man, only the black rain out of the bruised and swollen clouds all through the bitter black of night is fit atmosphere in such a land. The rain drives on, the stinking mud becomes more evilly yellow, the shell holes fill up with green-white water, the roads and tracks are covered in inches of slime, the black dying trees ooze and sweat and the shells never cease. They alone plunge overhead, tearing away the rotting tree stumps, breaking the plank roads, striking down horses and mules, annihilating, maiming, maddening, they plunge into the grave which is this land; one huge grave, and cast up on it the poor dead. It is unspeakable, godless, hopeless. I am no longer an artist interested and curious, I am a messenger who will bring back word from the men who are fighting to those who want the war to go on for ever. Feeble, inarticulate, will be my message, but it will have a bitter truth, and may it burn their lousy souls.

Paul Nash (1889–1946) after studying art at the Slade School in London mainly painted landscapes until the outbreak of war when he volunteered for the Artists' Rifles. It was not until the First World War that Nash fully realized himself as an artist. The scenes of desolation and violence on the battlefields of Flanders were a great stimulus to his artistic imagination. While convalescing in England in 1917, he exhibited his drawings at the Goupil gallery in London. The exhibition was a great success, and with the support of other artists and influential friends he was seconded to the Ministry of Information as an official war artist, and returned to France in November 1917.

In 1933 Nash founded 'Unit One', a group of painters and designers, and he was a member of the committee of the first international surrealist exhibition, which was held in London in 1936 and at which he exhibited. In the Second World War he was again appointed as official war artist and attached to the Royal Air Force.

'Sunrise. Inverness Copse.' Another of Paul Nash's war pictures, painted at the Front Line in 1917–1918.

ERNST LUDWIG KIRCHNER TO NELE VAN DE VELDE

Frauenkirch, 13 October 1918

Dear Fräulein Nele,

Warmest thanks for your letter of 4 October. You don't need to thank me for the woodcuts, for I sent them to you *en récompense* for yours. It's such a pity you didn't come here this summer, you would certainly have found a lot of interesting subjects to draw. And there was a room all ready for you in a hut.

Just watch the people closely as they move about picking the grapes. Down there it's still summer, I suppose, whereas our sun is already gilding the mountains and the larches are turning yellow, but the colours are wonderful, like old, dark red satin. Down here in the valley the huts stand out in the strongest Paris blue against the yellow fields. Here one really learns the values of the individual colours for the first time. And the harsh, monumental lines of the mountains. It is infinitely peaceful. In the Bündner room, which is so comfortable and warm, I am now trying to carry my unskilful paintings a bit further. I should really be very much interested to see some pictures by you in colour sometime.

Do you ever hear anything about French painters? I have seen no art of any kind for a long time, and would very much like to see some

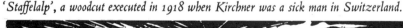

'*Staffelalp*', *a woodcut executed in 1918 when Kirchner was a sick man in Switzerland.*

more reproductions, particularly of Seurat, I still haven't been able to get hold of anything by him.

Otherwise the solitude and peace are doing me a lot of good. I have to lie down more in the autumn now, because of my illness. So I occupy myself with memories and paint better pictures in my thoughts than I can in real life.

I should so much like to help you to arrange things at Uttwil, but with my legs I should probably only get in the way. I look forward very much to seeing you again when I go back down there, and seeing the work you have done this summer. Where can you have found that beautiful Japan paper, it takes the printing ink wonderfully. You should try the English presses at Uttwil sometime, perhaps one can print small engravings on them too. Do you know, that lovely thin stone got broken unfortunately, and I shall now have to look round for a sub⁄stitute. I wasn't able to do much on it. When it comes to engraving I always reach out for a wood⁄block. That gives me the surest lines.

Warmest greetings, today and always,

from your
E. Kirchner

ERNST LUDWIG KIRCHNER TO HENRY VAN DE VELDE

Frauenkirch, 5 July 1919

Dear Monsieur van de Velde,
Many thanks for your kind letter. I would like to reply in the same elegant language, but I am afraid you would not much enjoy my unpractised French.

Alas, alas, you are mistaken in supposing that things have taken a turn for the better with me. In the last few weeks I have again suffered so much that I often felt it was not worth being alive. The happiness of being with you may have temporarily distracted my thoughts from my suffering, but it keeps on returning, as violent as ever.

I am very happy and thankful to be *here* and to remain. Here I can at least work a little on my good days, and be at peace among these simple, kindly people. In this solitude I have fought my way through to the possibility of continuing to live, even suffering so much. My time for circuses, *cocottes* and company is over. I made what I could out of it, and I do not think it had been done in that way before. Otherwise there is nothing to link me with those *événements*.

During my 7 years in Berlin I let the whole essence of that kind of thing seep into me so thoroughly that I now know it back to front, and can leave it. Now I have other tasks, and they lie here. In that respect our paths and aims are poles apart. You, the worldly-wise architect, receptive to every stimulus, I the man of one idea, the painter seeking forms for inner experiences. I do not know if you see what I mean.

I can only thank you for showing so much interest in me and my work, and beg that you will continue to do so.

I cannot go down again into the throng. I am more than ever afraid of crowds. But more still, my work here is only at the beginning of its possibilities. And I must try to do it, if I am to get any happiness at all out of life.

In August I shall be up in the Alps again. I probably shan't go up till the beginning of August, because I cannot walk very well at present. It would be wonderful if you and Nele could come up. One can quite well remain up there till the beginning of October.

Warmest greetings and good wishes to you and Nele,

Ever yours,
E. L. Kirchner

ERNST LUDWIG KIRCHNER TO NELE VAN DE VELDE

Dear Fräulein Nele,

Papa has just left, much to my regret, so now I must hurry to write you a few words.

Looking over some old drawings we came across a lot of copies from Indian wall-paintings. Papa thought you ought to see a book by John Griffith, *Paintings in the Indian Cave Temples of Candia Haber*, it would give you some suggestions. Unfortunately I haven't got it, but to give you some slight idea of the work I will send you tomorrow the very bad copies I made from it. And a few sketches from other exotics.

'Large Mountain Landscape with Meadow', a woodcut by Kirchner dating from 1933.

I took up those works many years ago. The originals are so strong and delicate that they defeat all attempts to copy them. Perhaps you feel, as I so much hope, that something comes to life in your figures. Papa calls it *du corps*. One might also say *sensibilité*, perhaps. We Europeans have to toil to achieve it, at least as a transitional stage, for it is what we feed our dreams upon. These Orientals have it in their blood, perhaps because they spend their lives in the sun. We poor wretched Europeans must sacrifice body and soul for even a shadow of it. Take the copies in exchange for your drawings from the Ethnographical Museum at Basle, which gave me a lot of pleasure in the winter. If one wishes to gain any profit from a work of art one must observe it and draw it just as one does nature itself, for in such a study one expresses one's feelings for one of its 1,000 facets, and through study real life enters into one's own being. It is not a question of trying to reproduce objective features, only of good practice for the fingers and for the perceptive faculty, and that too is very useful. You must have read how Van Gogh was always getting his brother to send him drawings to copy. And how Rembrandt used to copy Indian and Italian pictures. Not, of course, because they were short of material, but to get *du corps*. So one should be always drawing, everything that makes an impression, pictures, statues, objects, people, animals, nature – everything, everything, for it is just as difficult to develop one's own style in art as for a baby to learn to walk. One can

225

'Then comes the great battle with oneself.' This 'Self-portrait by the Window' shows Kirchner at work in 1920, soon after he had settled in Switzerland.

see from other people how it happens, but one has to do it for oneself.

As one climbs the ladder of one's own development, one can always find, among the world's infinite wealth of art, people with parallel sensibilities (one discovers them through one's feelings, when one sees something one likes), and to penetrate them by drawing them helps one to see oneself more clearly and thus prepares one for the next step.

You found parallel sensitivity in the Japanese, but you are trying for much more, and the little lithos breathe so much more freedom and warmth. Dream forms, with their gracile limbs, are not shown in the round. Oh, you'd love the Indians. The pure, Aryan Indians, not those one could see in Berlin, whose forms had become rigid and sterile through mingling with the Chinese. I am sorry I can only give you these botched sketches of them, and after all it is my feelings they reflect.

226

'The Circus', by Kirchner, painted in 1912. The subject appears often in his work, part of his attempt to express 'the richness and the joy of living'.

Your own impression would be quite different. They are perfectly flat, and yet absolute bodies, so that they have completely solved the mystery of painting. Yet one cannot imitate them. Not even their direct descendants were able to make simple copies. That has been tried. Their influence is apt to turn a European to sculpture, and that can only be avoided by carving figures from wood. Even working in three dimensions one automatically treats the surfaces as two-dimensional curves. If you trace those curves again in the human form, you are carried back to the origins, to the spiritual life expressed in these forms and folds. Then comes the great battle with oneself, the struggle to express this in forms, and that brings us to our own real task.

There's rather a lot of theory in all this, so forgive these last lines. But I have become a bit clumsy at explaining things.

ERNST LUDWIG KIRCHNER TO NELE VAN DE VELDE

Frauenkirch, 29 November 1920

Dear Nele,

But I can only do that if you drop the Herr too. I'm no Herr, as you would realize if you could see me washing up and sweeping. Many thanks for your letter and the Gauguin woodcuts, which interested me very much. Yes, the horse is a really beautiful woodcut, with all the soft ness of Gauguin's line. The other, it seems to me, doesn't quite come off. But that happens to all of us. Doesn't it look as though G. had used pear wood? But perhaps tropical wood, cut with the grain, also pro duces these delicate little lines that the horse has on its head and legs. One can see, incidentally, that Gauguin had Persian miniatures, Indian batik and Chinese art in his very blood. The shapes of the birds and the horse show that clearly. But although it looks very well, Gauguin can't stimulate us present day artists much. We need a direct route from life to plastic form. And we get it by perpetually drawing everything we see.

The paintbox arrived safely too, it is quite charming. But I must give it back to you when you come here again next summer. You mustn't part with it, that would never do. It is sufficient pleasure to me to have its help for the first brush drawings. At the moment I was making woodcuts from some designs I drew on the blocks this summer.

I am very much alone now, I don't want to go back to O. any more since I discovered how completely my ways and my life are mis interpreted. From the standpoint of people like that there is no way of access to our free, natural attitude to life. How could they possibly understand a pure, artistic being like you! How poor such people are, with their narrow circle of feelings, and how little they make of the infinite wealth and freedom life has to offer!

Thank you many times for your kind welcome to my wife, she wrote saying what a lovely time she had with you, and she was delighted with the pendant you gave her. Nothing makes her so happy as when friends show that they like her. So the summer will be lovely, because you must come, Nele, I have so much still to tell you and show you. Until then, draw wherever and however you can, take everything life has to offer.

You, too, find release only in art, you are one of those privileged people who have that gift, and you will be free and at peace so long as you make use of it. Art gives us an inner superiority, for it has scope for every sensation of which human beings are capable, and first and foremost for love, which is the basis of knowledge. The artist loves without wanting to possess, and no one on earth can understand that except other artists, that is why other people think us mad. It would be interesting to get at a definition of the word 'unhealthy', as applied by certain people to anything new; it is particularly the fashion nowadays. I won't try to answer the question of whether it is 'healthier' to paint a nude with no breasts or behind if the fingers on the hands are defined, but from the artistic point of view it is necessary in any case. The spectator shows what sort of person he is, if he is shocked by such things. I have found two more pulls of your woodcuts here. Your way of seeing and cutting is so different from mine that only deliberate malice could suggest you had come under my influence. I do not think anyone who did *not* know you had been here could discover such a thing.

I am excited about what you will do next. I would gladly come to Basle, write to me when you get there. I should be delighted to look at all the beautiful things there with you. Tomorrow I will send you a parcel of Eilido colours, Scholl stocks them too, in Holland as well. The two Gauguins I enclose with this letter.

Now you must forget that past weakness, once and for all, because you are a healthy, spontaneous person, don't be led astray by others. Go your own way, one cannot look to anyone for guidance in such a matter or one begins to hesitate. It will be delightful if you are here again next summer. In the meantime, make a lot of drawings from life of your brothers and sisters, bathing or whatever they happen to be doing. I hope by next summer to find something for you to work from. It is so important.

My best greetings to your mother, and to you, with my thanks,

Ever your
E. L. Kirchner

Ernst Ludwig Kirchner (1880–1938), the German painter and graphic artist, was one of the founder-members of 'Die Brücke', the group formed at Dresden

with the object of 'renewing German art'. He was in close touch with the 'Blaue Reiter' artists and worked for a number of years in Berlin until he was called up in 1914. He was a prey to severe mental and nervous troubles which lasted the rest of his life and was soon discharged from the army. In 1917 he settled in Davos, Switzerland, which was his home until his suicide in 1938. He was on very friendly terms with the architect and designer, Henry van de Velde, and his daughter Nele, with whom he corresponded frequently and at length.

Kirchner was acknowledged as a leading figure in the German Expressionist movement. In his great pre-war Berlin period he painted mainly city scenes but in Switzerland he turned to mountain and peasant subjects, but still in his highly-charged Expressionist manner. His style developed out of his study of primitive art and drew its strength from a vigorous handling of colour. His aim, as he himself put it, was to render visible objects as 'symbols expressing a reality experienced and discerned to the very source of its energy.' Kirchner also did important graphic work, principally woodcuts.

'The Waterfall' (1919). The scenery of Switzerland made a powerful impression on Kirchner and he produced a series of mountain studies that reflect it through his own intensely personal vision.

Giorgio de Chirico's 'Place d'Italie', an exploration of 'the most secret recesses of [the artist's] being'.

GIORGIO DE CHIRICO ON MYSTERY AND CREATION

1913

To become truly immortal a work of art must escape all human limits: logic and common sense will only interfere. But once these barriers are broken it will enter the regions of childhood vision and dream.

Profound statements must be drawn by the artist from the most secret recesses of his being; there no murmuring torrent, no birdsong, no rustle of leaves can distract him.

What I hear is valueless; only what I see is living, and when I close my eyes my vision is even more powerful.

It is most important that we should rid art of all that it has contained of *recognizable material* to date, all familiar subject matter, all traditional ideas, all popular symbols must be banished forthwith. More important still, we must hold enormous faith in ourselves: it is essential that the revelation we receive, the conception of an image which embraces a certain thing, which has no sense in itself, which has no subject, which means *absolutely nothing* from the logical point of view, I repeat, it is essential that such a revelation or conception should speak so strongly in us, evoke such agony or joy, that we feel compelled to paint, compelled by an impulse even more urgent than the hungry desperation which drives a man to tearing at a piece of bread like a savage beast.

I remember one vivid winter's day at Versailles. Silence and calm reigned supreme. Everything gazed at me with mysterious, questioning eyes. And then I realized that every corner of the palace, every column, every window possessed a spirit, an impenetrable soul. I looked around at the marble heroes, motionless in the lucid air, beneath the frozen rays of that winter sun which pours down on us *without love*, like perfect song. A bird was warbling in a window cage. At that moment I grew aware of the mystery which urges men to create certain strange forms. And the creation appeared more extraordinary than the creators.

Perhaps the most amazing sensation passed on to us by prehistoric man is that of presentiment. It will always continue. We might consider it as an eternal proof of the irrationality of the universe. Original man must have wandered through a world full of uncanny signs. He must have trembled at each step.

Giorgio de Chirico was born in Greece in 1888 of Italian parents. His father was an engineer, and he himself originally studied engineering and attended the Athens Polytechnic. In 1905 he went to Munich and studied art, and was influenced by Böcklin and Klinger. He stayed in Italy from 1908 to 1910 and went to Paris in 1911 where he met Picasso and the poet and avant-garde critic Guillaume Apollinaire. In 1915 he returned to Italy and founded a new movement in painting with the Futurist painter Carlo Carrà, which they called 'Pittura Metafisica' (Metaphysical Painting). This new style, with its essentially romantic nature and the way in which Chirico's paintings suggest static, timeless dream-images, with their stage-like arrangement of objects and architectural elements, was a direct reaction against the 'dynamism' of the Futurists. In 1919, writing for the Italian art review 'Valori Plastici', Chirico published his basic concepts for a 'Metaphysical aesthetic':

GIORGIO DE CHIRICO ON A METAPHYSICAL AESTHETIC

1919

My mind was obsessed, and still is, by carpenters' squares: I saw them rising like strange planets behind all pictorial designs. . . .

The structure of cities, the architecture of houses, squares, gardens, public walks, gateways, railway stations, etc. – all these provide us with the basic principles of a great Metaphysical aesthetic. . . . We, who live under the sign of the Metaphysical alphabet, we know the joys and sorrows to be found in a gateway, a street corner, a room, on the surface of a table, between the sides of a box. . . .

Perfect knowledge of the space an object should occupy in a picture, and of the space that separates one object from another, establishes a new astronomy of things attached to our planet by the magic law of gravity. Canons of the Metaphysical aesthetic lie in the minutely-accurate and precisely-estimated use of surfaces and volumes. . . . We are building in paint a new Metaphysical psychology of things.

Chirico later abandoned his 'metaphysical' style to produce works directly inspired by the Old Masters, and ceased to have any more influence on the modern movement.

PIET MONDRIAAN TO THEO VAN DOESBURG

Dear Sir, *Amsterdam, 1915* (?)

As you see, this is a composition consisting of vertical and horizontal lines which will (in an abstract manner) have to express the idea of rising upwards, of magnitude. This is the same idea which used, for example, to be the guiding principle in the construction of cathedrals. Since only the manner of expression and not the representation has to express this general idea, I have not given any title. An abstract human mind will, of itself, receive the intended impression. I always confine myself to expressing the general, i.e. the intrinsic element (that which is closest to the spirit), doing this in the simplest external form, in order to be able to express in this way the inner meaning in the least veiled manner.

PIET MONDRIAAN TO THEO VAN DOESBURG

Dear Sir and Friend, *Amsterdam, 20 November 1915*

Forgive me for saying so, but good things just have to grow very slowly. I say this in connection with your plans, about which I heard from Loe Saalborn, for launching a journal. I do not think that the time is favourable for it. More must first be achieved in art in that direction. I hardly know anyone who is really creating art in our style, in other words, art which has arrived. In my opinion, you can achieve enough in *Eenheid* for the time being. There will not be sufficient material for a specific journal or it will be partially successful only (i.e. you will have to include in it what is not consistent with our ideas).

PIET MONDRIAAN IN THE FIRST ISSUE OF 'DE STIJL'

October 1917

The cultivated man of today is gradually turning away from natural things, and his life is becoming more and more abstract.

Natural (external) things become more and more automatic, and we observe that our vital attention fastens more and more on internal things.

The life of the truly modern man is neither purely materialistic nor purely emotional. It manifests itself rather as a more autonomous life of the human mind becoming conscious of itself.

Modern man – although a unity of body, mind and soul – exhibits a changed consciousness: every expression of his life has today a different aspect, that is, an aspect more positively abstract.

It is the same with art. Art will become the product of another duality in man: the product of a cultivated externality and of an inwardness deepened

'The straight line and the clearly defined primary colour': *Composition with Red, Yellow and Blue*.

and more conscious. As a pure representation of the human mind, art will express itself in an aesthetically purified, that is to say, abstract form.

The truly modern artist is aware of abstraction in an emotion of beauty; he is conscious of the fact that the emotion of beauty is cosmic, universal. This conscious recognition has for its corollary an abstract plasticism, for man adheres only to what is universal.

The new plastic idea cannot, therefore, take the form of a natural or concrete representation, although the latter does always indicate the universal to a degree, or at least conceals it within. This new plastic idea will ignore the particulars of appearance, that is to say, natural form and colour. On the contrary, it should find its expression in the abstraction of form and colour, that is to say, in the straight line and the clearly defined primary colour.

These universal means of expression were discovered in modern painting by a logical and gradual progress toward ever more abstract form and colour. Once the solution was discovered, there followed the exact representation of relations alone, that is to say, of the essential and fundamental element in any plastic emotion of the beautiful.

The new plastic idea thus correctly represents actual aesthetic relationships. To the modern artist, it is a natural consequence of all the plastic ideas of the past. This is particularly true of painting, which is the art least bound to contingencies. The picture can be a pure reflection of life in its deepest essence.

Piet Mondriaan (1872–1944) began his artistic career as a landscape painter before being attracted to Cubism after his arrival in Paris in 1911. During the First World War he returned to Holland, when his work attracted the attention of Theo van Doesburg, an active writer on avant-garde art and a painter himself. In 1917 he collaborated with Van Doesburg in the founding of a new magazine 'De Stijl' (Style), for which he contributed many important articles in which he first put forward his theories on Neo-Plasticism – a highly personal style of abstraction which he had evolved and which principally consisted in the use of rigid geometrical shapes and primary colours. In 1937 he summarized his theories in a book entitled 'Plastic Art and Pure Plastic Art'. Mondriaan spent the last years of his life in London and New York.

HENRI MATISSE TO HENRY CLIFFORD

Vence, 14 February 1948

Dear Mr Clifford,

I hope that my exhibition may be worthy of all the work it is making for you, which touches me deeply.

However, in view of the great repercussions it may have, seeing how much preparation has gone into it, I wonder whether its scope will not have a more or less unfortunate influence on young painters. How are they going to interpret the impression of apparent facility that they will get from a rapid, or even a superficial, overall view of my paintings and drawings?

I have always tried to hide my own efforts and wished my works to have the lightness and joyousness of a springtime which never lets anyone suspect the labours it has cost. So I am afraid that the young, seeing in my work only the apparent facility and negligence in the drawing, will use this as an excuse for dispensing with certain efforts which I believe necessary.

The few exhibitions that I have had the opportunity of seeing during these last years make me fear that the young painters are avoiding the slow and painful preparation which is necessary for the education of any contemporary painter who claims to construct by colour alone.

Matisse's early works, like this 'Nude with Pipes' of 1906, are revealing in their strict, almost academic, discipline. They illustrate the point made in the letter, that his 'apparent facility and negligence in the drawing' are rooted in 'slow and painful preparation'.

This slow and painful work is indispensable. Indeed, if gardens were not dug over at the proper time, they would soon be good for nothing. Do we not first have to clear, and then cultivate, the ground at each season of the year?

When an artist does not know how to prepare his flowering period, by work which bears little resemblance to the final result, he has a short future before him; or when an artist who has 'arrived' no longer feels the necessity of getting back to earth from time to time, he begins to go round in circles repeating himself, until by this very repetition, his curiosity is extinguished.

An artist must possess Nature. He must identify himself with her rhythm, by efforts that will prepare the mastery which will later enable him to express himself in his own language.

The future painter must feel what is useful for his development – drawing or even sculpture – everything that will let him become one with Nature, identify himself with her, by entering into the things – which is what I call Nature – that arouse his feelings. I believe study by means of drawing is most essential. If drawing is of the Spirit and colour

'Reclining Odalisque' by Matisse, a painting that typifies his feeling for rich sensuous line. In 1910 he had seen the exhibition of Near Eastern art at Munich and had been fascinated by the brilliant decorative qualities of the works shown.

The 'Odalisque' became a theme to which Matisse returned again and again, making it – with his arabesque patterns and pure light colours – peculiarly his own.

of the Senses, you must draw first, to cultivate the spirit and to be able to lead colour into spiritual paths. That is what I want to cry aloud, when I see the work of the young men for whom painting is no longer an adventure, and whose only goal is the impending first one-man show which will first start them on the road to fame.

It is only after years of preparation that the young artist should touch colour – not colour as description, that is, but as a means of intimate expression. Then he can hope that all the images, even all the symbols, which he uses, will be the reflection of his love for things, a reflection in which he can have confidence if he has been able to carry out his education, with purity, and without lying to himself. Then he will employ colour with discernment. He will place it in accordance with a natural

239

design, unformulated and completely concealed, that will spring directly from his feelings; this is what allowed Toulouse-Lautrec, at the end of his life, to exclaim, 'At last, I do not know how to draw any more.'

The painter who is just beginning thinks that he paints from his heart. The artist who has completed his development also thinks that he paints from his heart. Only the latter is right, because his training and discipline allow him to accept impulses that he can, at least partially, conceal.

I do not claim to teach; I only want my exhibition not to suggest false interpretations to those who have their own way to make. I should like people to know that they cannot approach colour as if coming into a barn door: that one must go through a severe preparation to be worthy of it. But first of all, it is clear that one must have a gift for colour as a singer must have a voice. Without this gift one can get nowhere, and not everyone can declare like Corregio, '*Anch'io son pittore.*' A colourist makes his presence known even in a simple charcoal drawing.

My dear Mr Clifford, here is the end of my letter. I started it to let you know that I realize the trouble you are taking over me at the moment. I see that, obeying an interior necessity, I have made it an expression of what I feel about drawing, colour and the importance of discipline in the education of an artist. If you think that all these reflec-tions of mine can be of any use to anyone, do whatever you think best with this letter . . .

Please believe me, dear Mr Clifford,

Yours gratefully,
Henri Matisse

Henri Matisse (1869–1954), the son of a corn-chandler in northern France, was intended for a legal career, but turned to painting, studied in Paris under Bouguereau and Gustave Moreau, and became friendly with Derain and Rouault, with whom he exhibited at the Salon d'Automne in 1905. A critic dubbed them 'wild beasts in a cage' and the group became known as 'Les Fauves'. Matisse, on the contrary, claimed that his guiding principles were calm, balance and purity; he wanted his art to have a soothing, healing influence and ignored problematical subjects. Even after he had gained celebrity he continued to make copies of masterpieces in the Louvre and his flat contained a choice selection of Cézanne watercolours, studies by Courbet, and examples of Indian and Moslem art. He was fond of teaching and had a large circle of pupils; he was also a prolific writer on art, though he sometimes ironically quoted his own early remark that 'anyone who decides to sell his soul to painting had better begin by biting off his tongue'. In his own opinion the culmination of his work was reached with the Chapelle du Rosaire which he designed for the Dominican nuns at Vence and which was consecrated in 1951. He used to say it was not a work he had chosen, but one allotted to him by fate towards the close of his life, and that it had enabled him to achieve something for which he had been seeking.

A view of the interior of the chapel at Vence that Matisse decorated in his old age, designing not only the murals but all the furniture, the altar, and the crucifix as well.

PIERRE BONNARD TO M. TÉRIADE IN CONVERSATION

Le Cannet, 1942

A picture is a succession of blobs that connect up and finally compose the subject, the piece over which the eye can stray without a hitch. The beauty of a piece of ancient marble is constituted by a whole series of movements the fingers are compelled to make.

The virtuosos knew that their subjects ought to be written out in full. But their means were not always honest. Oil painting as a medium gave opportunity for a succession of tones which were sometimes hollow. Titian would make the whole length of an arm with a drop of paint. Whereas Cézanne wanted all his transitions to be conscious tones. But one should not condemn transparency outright. One should reject anything excessive. Rembrandt used transparency, but what transparency!

Not everything you see sends you into transports of joy. One is struck by very agreeable relationships that painters seize upon and put into their painting. For beauty can be extracted from everything.

I approved of collages when they were serving a plastic aim, that is to say, when they were introducing a real substance, external to painting, which, from its very nature, from this very fact, recalled the artificial in painting. For instance I have a particular affection for the gilded and patterned backgrounds used by primitive painters and illuminators, and for the way they introduced coats of arms and heraldic devices into their pictures.

PIERRE BONNARD IN CONVERSATION WITH ANGÈLE LAMOTTE

1943

I tried to paint it [a bunch of roses] directly, precisely, I let myself become involved in details, I let myself drift into painting roses. I found that I was floundering, that I was getting nowhere, I had lost and could not recover my original idea, the vision that had charmed me, the starting-point. I hope I can get it back – by rediscovering that first charm.

The painting of a bunch of roses was for Bonnard a complex psychological process.

I often see interesting things around me, but for me to want to paint them they must have a particular charm – beauty – one can call it beauty. While I paint them I try not to lose control over the original idea, I am weak, and if I let myself go, as I did with the bunch of roses, after a moment I have lost what I saw at first and I no longer know where I am making for.

The presence of the object, the motif, is a great embarrassment to the painter while he is actually painting. The starting-point of a picture is an idea – if the object is there while one is working, there is always a danger that the artist may be captivated by the implications of the direct, immediate view, and lose the original idea as he goes on. So that after working for a time the painter can no longer recapture the idea he started with, and begins to rely on what is fortuitous, he paints the shadows as he sees them, tries to describe certain shadows he notices, or some detail that did not strike him at first.

'So you never work from the motif?'

Yes I do, but I leave it, I go to check by it, I come back, I return a little later, I do not let myself become absorbed by the object itself. I paint alone in my studio, I do everything in my studio. In short there is a conflict between the original idea, which is the right one, the one in the painter's mind, and the variable, varied world of the subject, the motif, which prompted the first inspiration.

There have been very few painters who could tackle the motif directly – and those who got away with it had their own personal methods of self-defence. Cézanne approached a subject with a firm idea of what he wanted to do, and he took from nature only what fitted in with his idea. He would often sit there, basking in the sun like a lizard, without even touching a brush. He could wait until things went back to being as they were in his conception of them. Of all painters he was the most strongly armed for dealing with nature, the purest, the most sincere.

Renoir painted Renoirs first and foremost. He often had models with dull complexions, not pearly, and he painted them pearly. He used the model for a movement, a shape, but he did not copy, he never lost the idea of what he could do. One day I was out walking with him and he said, 'Bonnard, one must embellish.' By 'embellish' he meant the share the artist has to bring to his picture in the first place.

Claude Monet used to paint from the motif, but only for ten minutes. He did not allow time for things to capture him. He would come back to work again when the light was as it had been the first time. He knew how to wait – he kept several pictures going at once.

The Impressionists went out to the motif, but they were better de-fended from the actual object than other painters, because of their methods, their ways of painting. With Pissarro it is even more visible, he used to rearrange things – there is more system in his painting. Seurat did only tiny studies from nature, all the rest was composed in his studio.

'Self-portrait' by Pierre Bonnard, painter of domesticity, of 'intimism'.

You can easily see the difference between the painters who could defend themselves and those who surrendered to their subject if you go to the Prado and compare the paintings of Titian and Velazquez. Titian's defence was total, all his pictures bear his mark, they were carried out in accordance with his original idea. Whereas with Velazquez there are great differences in quality between the subjects that charmed him, such as his portraits of infantas, and his big academic compositions where there is nothing to be seen but the actual models, the actual objects, with no trace of preliminary inspiration.

Through charm, or the preliminary idea, the painter achieves universality. It is charm that decides the choice of subject and corresponds precisely to the painting. If this charm, this preliminary idea, fades away, nothing is left but the motif, the object, which thrusts itself upon the painter and dominates him. After that, his painting is no longer his. With some painters – Titian, for instance – the charm is so strong that it never deserts them, even if they remain for a very long time in direct contact with their subject. Personally, I am very weak, it is difficult for me to control myself when face to face with my subject.

Pierre Bonnard (1867–1947) painted slowly and meticulously and some of his paintings are the result of work done at intervals over a long period of months. He would put aside one picture for another, only resuming work on it when he had fully decided on the next step in its creation. He also had a habit of leaving a picture when it was nearly completed in order to give himself time to see it again with a fresh vision, and to modify it if he thought necessary.

Bonnard had studied art in his spare time, while taking a degree in law. After he had decided to paint full-time he earned his living at first by designing posters and lithographs. He was for a while a member of the French group of painters who called themselves 'Les Nabis' after the Hebrew word for 'prophet', and was strongly influenced by Gauguin and Japanese colour-prints. After 1905 he left Paris to live mainly in the country where his work became more impressionistic in technique and use of colour. In 1926 he settled in Le Cannet, a suburb of Cannes, where he made his home for the rest of his life.

Besides painting, Bonnard undertook large-scale decorations, made many etchings and lithographs, and illustrated books.

GINO SEVERINI ON FUTURISM AND CUBISM

1956

In our young days, when Modigliani and I first came to Paris, in 1906, nobody was very clear about ideas. But unconsciously, we knew quite a lot of things, of which we became aware later on.

It was during the first few years that we realized the presence of a dualism deep down within us, where another person, whom we ourselves do not know, tends, at the moment of the creative act, to supplant the person we believe ourselves to be and would like to be. It is difficult to bring these two individualities into accord, yet it is upon their accord that the development of a personality largely depends.

My first contact with the art of Seurat, whom I adopted, once and for all, as my master, did a great deal to help me to express myself in terms of the two simultaneous and often opposed aspirations. This opposition caused me much mental torture, I must admit, but since then I have found consolation in W. Blake. 'Without Contraries is no progression', he says in his *Proverbs of Hell*. And Baudelaire's idea that 'Variety is an essential condition of life' seems to me to be in perfect accord with my aspirations and with my intention, as a Futurist painter, to put *life* in the place occupied by *reasoning* in the art of the Cubist period.

'. . . a person who is seated, or an inanimate object, though apparently static, could be considered dynamically and suggest dynamic forms', *wrote Severini*, 'I may mention as an example the "Portrait of Madame S."'

In the early days the Cubists' method of grasping an object was to go round and round it; the Futurists declared that one had to get inside it. In my opinion the two views can be reconciled in a poetic cognition of the world. But through the very fact that they appealed to the creative depths in the painter by awakening in him hidden forces which were intuitive and vitalizing, the Futurist theories did more than the Cubist principles to open up unexplored and boundless horizons.

The intellectual abstraction of the second period of Cubism was of great importance, however. By its aspiration to the *eternal* and its 'concept of proportion inspired by the Classics', it revived the sense of *craftmanship* in many painters. And this perfectly coincided with another of my ambitions – which was to make, with paint, an object having the same perfection of craftsmanship that a cabinet-maker would put into a piece of furniture.

People have often taken a negative view of the decorative and ornamental possibilities offered by Cubism. This is a great mistake; Cubism was capable of giving rise to *mural art* and *applied art* of great artistic and historical importance; and a few artists, including myself, have proved as much.

It should also be borne in mind that the research on *movement* and the dynamic outlook on the world, which were the bases of Futurist theory, in no way required one to paint nothing but speeding cars or ballerinas in action, for a person who is seated, or an inanimate object, though apparently static, could be considered dynamically and suggest dynamic forms. I may mention as an example the 'Portrait of Madame S.', of 1912, and the 'Seated Woman', of 1914.

The purpose of these regrettably limited reflections is to help those who may wish to investigate my work thoroughly, either from the point of view of Futurism or from that of Cubism. Futurism and Cubism are comparable in importance to the invention of perspective, for which they substituted a new concept of space. All subsequent movements were latent in them or brought about by them.

In conclusion, my opinion is that the two movements cannot be regarded as in opposition to each other, even though they started from opposite points; I maintain (an idea approved by Apollinaire and later by Matisse) that they are two extremes of the same sign, tending to coincide at certain points which only the poetic instinct of the painter can discover: *poetry* being the content and *raison d'être* of art.

Gino Severini was born in Cortona in 1883 and came to Paris in 1906, the same year as Modigliani. He was at first greatly influenced by Seurat's theories on light and the division of colours, and in 1910 he signed the manifesto of the Futurist painters, together with his fellow Italians, Boccioni, Carrà and Balla. He soon reacted against the movement, regarding it as too rhetorical, and became attracted towards Cubism, which had a greater intellectual appeal for him. After a few years in which his style approached that of the Cubists, and after various periods of experimentation with figurative art he reverted to abstract forms. In recent years Severini has also decorated several churches in Switzerland with frescoes and mosaics.

'Seated Woman' of 1914 is the other picture mentioned by Severini in his letter. The emphasis on movement in Futurist theory did not limit the painter to the depiction of objects actually moving.

HENRY MOORE IN AN ARTICLE 'THE SCULPTOR SPEAKS'

18 August 1937

Since the Gothic, European sculpture had become overgrown with moss, weeds – all sorts of surface excrescences which completely concealed shape. It has been Brancusi's special mission to get rid of this overgrowth, and to make us once more shape-conscious. To do this he has had to concentrate on very simple direct shapes, to keep his sculpture, as it were, one-cylindered, to refine and polish a single shape to a degree almost too precious. Brancusi's work, apart from its individual value, has been of historical importance in the development of contemporary sculpture. But it may now be no longer necessary to close down and restrict sculpture to the single (static) form unit. We can now begin to open out. To relate and combine together several forms of varied sizes, sections, and directions into one organic whole.

Although it is the human figure which interests me most deeply, I have always paid great attention to natural forms, such as bones, shells, and pebbles, etc. Sometimes for several years running I have been to the same part of the sea-shore – but each year a new shape of pebble has caught my eye, which the year before, though it was there in hundreds, I never saw. Out of the millions of pebbles passed in walking along the shore, I choose out to see with excitement only those which fit in with my existing form-interest at the time. A different thing happens if I sit down and examine a handful one by one. I may then extend my form-experience more, by giving my mind time to become conditioned to a new shape.

There are universal shapes to which everybody is subconsciously conditioned and to which they can respond if their conscious control does not shut them off.

Pebbles show Nature's way of working stone. Some of the pebbles I pick up have holes right through them.

When first working direct in a hard and brittle material like stone, the lack of experience and great respect for the material, the fear of ill-treating it, too often result in relief surface carving, with no sculptural power.

But with more experience the completed work in stone can be kept within the limitations of its material, that is, not be weakened beyond its natural constructive build and yet be turned from an inert mass into a composition which has a full form existence, with masses of varied sizes and sections working together in spatial relationship.

A piece of stone can have a hole through it and not be weakened – if the hole is of a studied size, shape and direction. On the principle of the arch, it can remain just as strong.

The first hole made through a piece of stone is a revelation.

The hole connects one side to the other, making it immediately more three-dimensional.

A hole can itself have as much shape-meaning as a solid mass.

Sculpture in air is possible, where the stone contains only the hole, which is the intended and considered form.

The mystery of the hole – the mysterious fascination of caves in hill-sides and cliffs.

Henry Moore: 'Two Forms' – but combined into 'one organic whole'.

There is a right physical size for every idea.

Pieces of good stone have stood about my studio for long periods, because though I've had ideas which would fit their proportions and materials perfectly, their size was wrong.

There is a size to scale not to do with its actual physical size, its measurement in feet and inches – but connected with vision.

A carving might be several times over life size and yet be petty and small in feeling – and a small carving only a few inches in height can give the feeling of huge size and monumental grandeur, because the vision behind it is big. Example, Michelangelo's drawings or a Masaccio Madonna – and the Albert Memorial.

For Henry Moore the proportions, the texture and the size of the material must be 'right' for the idea. This 'Half Figure' of 1931 is in veined alabaster.

In his 'Reclining Figure' of 1939 Moore achieves a monumental effect on a human scale.

Yet actual physical size has an emotional meaning. We relate every-thing to our own size, and our emotional response to size is controlled by the fact that men on the average are between five and six feet high.

An exact model to one-tenth scale of Stonehenge, where the stones would be less than us, would lose all its impressiveness.

Sculpture is more affected by actual size considerations than painting. A painting is isolated by a frame from its surroundings (unless it serves just a decorative purpose) and so retains more easily its own imaginary scale.

If practical considerations allowed me, cost of material, of transport, etc., I should like to work on large carvings more often than I do. The average in-between size does not disconnect an idea enough from prosaic everyday life. The very small or the very big takes on an added size emotion.

Recently I have been working in the country, where, carving in the open air, I find sculpture more natural than in a London studio, but it needs bigger dimensions. A large piece of stone or wood placed almost anywhere at random in a field, orchard, or garden, immediately looks right and inspiring.

My drawings are done mainly as a help towards making sculpture – as a means of generating ideas for sculpture, tapping oneself for the initial idea; and as a way of sorting out ideas and developing them.

Also, sculpture compared with drawing is a slow means of expression, and I find drawing a useful outlet for ideas which there is not time enough to realize as sculpture. And I use drawing as a method of study and observation of natural forms (drawings from life, drawings of bones, shells, etc.).

And I sometimes draw just for its own enjoyment.

Experience though has taught me that the difference there is between drawing and sculpture should not be forgotten. A sculptural idea which may be satisfactory as a drawing always needs some alteration when translated into sculpture.

At one time whenever I made drawings for sculpture I tried to give them as much the illusion of real sculptures as I could – that is, I drew by the method of illusion, of light falling on a solid object. But now I find that carrying a drawing so far that it becomes a substitute for the sculpture either weakens the desire to do the sculpture, or is likely to make the sculpture only a dead realization of the drawing.

I now leave a wider latitude in the interpretation of the drawings I make for sculpture, and draw often in line and flat tones without the light and shade illusion of three dimensions; but this does not mean that the vision behind the drawing is only two-dimensional.

The violent quarrel between the abstractionists and the surrealists seems to me quite unnecessary. All good art has contained both abstract and surrealist elements, just as it has contained both classical and romantic elements – order and surprise, intellect and imagination, conscious and unconscious. Both sides of the artist's personality must play their part. And I think the first inception of a painting or a sculpture may begin from either end. As far as my own experience is concerned, I sometimes begin a drawing with no preconceived problem to solve, with only the desire to use pencil on paper, and make lines, tones, and shapes with no conscious aim; but as my mind takes in what is so produced, a point arrives where some idea becomes conscious and crystallizes, and then a control and ordering begin to take place.

Henry Moore was born in Yorkshire in 1898 in a miner's family and originally intended to become a schoolmaster. After serving in the First World War, in which he was injured by poison gas, he began to study art at Leeds, then at the Royal College of Art in London, where he was later offered a teaching post. He also taught at the Chelsea Art School and began to travel extensively in Europe. During the Second World War he produced a series of drawings of life in the London air raid shelters which revealed his powers as a draughtsman to a public that was still largely puzzled by his sculpture. He has undertaken many official commissions, particularly since the war, such as those for the new UNESCO building in Paris and for English churches and war memorials, and has won international recognition as the outstanding British sculptor of our time.

Moore has written sparingly on his work and artistic theories, most of his statements are in the form of notes, articles and radio broadcasts.

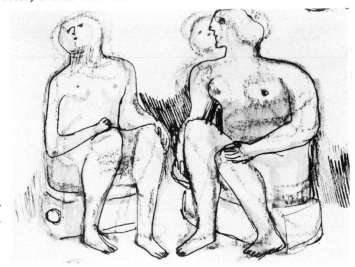

Moore's drawings are done either 'for enjoyment' or – more often – 'as a help towards making sculpture – as a means of generating ideas'. These 'Seated Figures', in chalk, pen and wash, date from 1932.

PABLO PICASSO TO CHRISTIAN ZERVOS IN CONVERSATION

Boisgeloup, winter 1934

Unfortunately for me – and perhaps fortunately for me – I place things according to my loves. What a sad fate for a painter who loves blondes, but who refrains from putting them in his picture because they don't go with the basket of fruit! What misery for a painter who hates apples to be obliged to use them all the time because they go with the cloth! I put everything I love into my pictures. So much the worse for the things, they have only to arrange themselves with one another.

Formerly pictures used to move towards completion in progressive stages. Each day would bring something new. A picture was a sum of additions. With me, a picture is a sum of destructions. I do a picture, then I destroy it. But in the long run nothing is lost; the red that I took away from one place turns up somewhere else.

It would be very curious to record by means of photographs, not the stages of a picture, but its metamorphoses. Perhaps one would perceive the path taken by a mind in order to put its dream into a concrete form. But what is really very curious is to observe that fundamentally the picture does not change, that despite appearances the initial vision remains almost intact. I often see a light and a shade, when I have put them in my picture I do my utmost to break them down by adding a colour which creates a contrary effect. When the work is photographed I per⁄ ceive that what I had introduced to correct my original vision disappears and that ultimately the impression given by the photograph corresponds to my original vision, prior to the transformations carried out by my will.

I would like to manage to prevent people from ever seeing how a picture of mine has been done. What can it possibly matter? What I want is that the only thing emanating from my picture should be emotion.

Abstract art is only painting. And what's so dramatic about that?

There is no abstract art. One must always begin with something. Afterwards one can remove all semblance of reality; there is no longer any danger as the idea of the object has left an indelible imprint. It is the object which aroused the artist, stimulated his ideas and set off his emotions. These ideas and emotions will be imprisoned in his work for good; whatever they do they will never be able to escape from the picture; they are an integral part of it, even though their presence can no longer be discerned. Whether he wants it or not, man is the instrument of nature; she imposes on him her character and appearance. In my paintings of Dinard, as in my paintings of Pourville, I have given expression to more or less the same vision. Yet you yourself have noticed, unaided, how different is the atmosphere of the pictures painted in Brittany and in Normandy, since you have recognized the light of the Dieppe cliffs. I didn't copy that light, I didn't pay any particular attention to it. I was simply bathed in it; my eyes had seen it and my subconscious recorded my vision; my hand preserved my sensations. You cannot go against nature. She is stronger than the strongest of men! We have every interest to be on good terms with her. We can permit ourselves some liberties; but in details only.

Neither is there figurative and non-figurative art. All things appear to us in the shape of forms. Even in metaphysics ideas are expressed by forms,

'The Bull' – simplified, transformed, reduced to the essential residue of a few expressive lines by Picasso in a space of five weeks. Four stages of a lithograph.

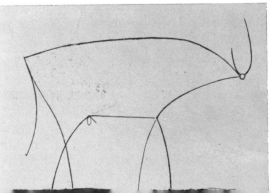

well then think how absurd it would be to think of painting without the imagery of forms. A figure, an object, a circle, are forms; they affect us more or less intensely. Some are closer to our feelings and give rise to emotions which concern our affective faculties; others appeal more particularly to the intellect. I must accept all of them, as my mind has as great a need of emotion as my senses. Do you think it interests me that this· painting represents two figures? These two figures existed, they exist no more. The sight of them gave me an initial emotion, little by little their real presence grew indistinct, they became a fiction for me, then they disappeared, or rather, were turned into problems of all kinds. For me they are no longer two figures but shapes and colours, don't misunderstand me, shapes and colours, though, that sum up the idea of the two figures and preserve the vibration of their existence.

The artist is a receptacle for emotions derived from anywhere: from the sky, from the earth, from a piece of paper, from a passing figure, from a spider's web. This is why one must not make a distinction between things. For them there are no aristocratic quarterings. One must take things where one finds them, except in one's own works. I have a horror of copying myself, but when I am shown a folder of old drawings, for example, I do not hesitate to take from them whatever I want.

When we did Cubist paintings, our intention was not to produce Cubist paintings but to express what was within us. No one laid down a course of action for us and our friends the poets followed our endeavour attentively but they never dictated it to us. Some young painters today frequently have the course they are to follow laid down for them, and apply themselves like good pupils to performing their task correctly.

The academic teaching on beauty is false. We have been misled, but so completely misled that we can no longer find so much as a shadow of a truth again. The beauties of the Parthenon, the Venuses, the Nymphs, the Narcissuses, are so many lies. Art is not the application of a canon of beauty, but what the instinct and the brain can conceive independently of that canon. When you love a woman you don't take instruments to measure her body, you love her with your desires, and yet people have done their utmost to introduce a canon even into love. To tell the truth the Parthenon is only a truss on which a roof has been placed; colonnades and sculptures were added because there were people in Athens who worked and who wanted to express themselves. It is not what the artist does that counts, but what he is. Cézanne would never have interested me if he had lived and thought like Jacques-Émile Blanche, even if the apple he had painted had been ten times more beautiful. What interests us is the anxiety of Cézanne, the teaching of Cézanne, the anguish of Van Gogh, in short the inner drama of the man. The rest is false.

Everyone wants to understand painting. Why don't they try to understand the song of the birds? Why do they love a night, a flower, everything which surrounds man, without attempting to understand them? Whereas where painting is concerned, they want to understand. Let them understand above all that the artist works from necessity; that he, too, is a minute element of the world to whom one should

'. . . little by little . . . they [the subject] disappeared, or rather, were turned into problems of all kinds.' *Picasso's observation can be applied to his 'Farmer's Wife on a Stepladder', where this process obviously took place. It was painted in 1933.*

ascribe no more importance than to so many things in nature which charm us but which we do not explain to ourselves. Those who attempt to explain a picture are on the wrong track most of the time. Gertrude Stein, overjoyed, told me some time ago that she had finally understood what my picture represented: three musicians. It was a still-life!

How can you expect a beholder to experience my picture as I experienced it? A picture comes to me a long time beforehand; who knows how long a time beforehand, I sensed, saw, and painted it and yet the next day even I do not understand what I have done. How can anyone penetrate my dreams, my instincts, my desires, my thoughts, which have taken a long time to fashion themselves and come to the surface, above all to grasp what I put there, perhaps involuntarily?

Pablo Picasso was born in Malaga in 1881, the son of a professor of drawing. He showed exceptional talent at an early age and was admitted to the advanced class at the Academy of Fine Arts at Barcelona when only fourteen. He first visited Paris in 1900, finally settling there four years later, and it was there, in 1907, after going through his naturalistic 'Blue' and 'Rose' periods, that he became influenced by Negro sculpture and Cézanne's later works and painted 'Les Demoiselles d'Avignon' – a work which marked a turning-point in his career and heralded a revolution in art. In this same year Picasso met Georges Braque and from 1909 they worked together to create a new pictorial idiom – Cubism. With the outbreak of war in 1914 the two artists separated and while continuing to paint near abstract works Picasso returned to a more naturalistic style and embarked on a series of monumental Neo-classical figure paintings. By 1923, however, another stylistic change had occurred, his figures becoming increasingly distorted and convulsive as he entered on his Metamorphic phase. Since then Picasso has introduced no major stylistic innovations but has played variations on these different styles moving from one to another, or combining them, with seemingly effortless facility. The most versatile and prolific artist of our time, Picasso has worked with dazzling success in a great number of artistic media in addition to painting and drawing, including lithography, etching, sculpture and ceramics. He has also produced book illustrations, designed costumes and décors for Diaghilev's Ballets Russes, and written poetry and a play.

MARC CHAGALL ON HIS ARRIVAL IN PARIS

In 1910, after choosing two pictures, Winawer gave me a monthly grant which enabled me to live in Paris.

I set off.

After four days I arrived in Paris.

Only the great distance which separates Paris from my birthplace kept me from returning there immediately or at least after a week, or a month.

I even wanted to invent some holiday or other just so as to be able to go back.

It was the Louvre that put an end to all these hesitations.

When I walked round the circular Veronese room and the rooms that the works of Manet, Delacroix and Courbet are in, I desired nothing more.

In my imagination Russia took the form of a basket suspended from a parachute. The deflated pear of the balloon was hanging down, growing cold and descending slowly in the course of the years.

This was how Russian art appeared to me, or something of the sort.

In fact whenever I thought or talked about Russian art I would experience the same troubled and confused emotions, full of bitterness and resentment.

It was as if Russian art had been fatally condemned to remain in the wake of the West.

If Russian painters were condemned to become the pupils of the West they were, I think, rather unfaithful ones by their very natures. The best Russian realist conflicts with the realism of Courbet.

The most authentic Russian Impressionism leaves one perplexed if one compares it with Monet and Pissarro.

Here, in the Louvre, before the canvases of Manet, Millet and others, I understood why my alliance with Russia and Russian art did not take root. Why my language itself is foreign to them.

Why people do not place confidence in me. Why the artistic circles fail to recognize me.

Why in Russia I am entirely useless.

And why everything I do seems strange to them and everything that they themselves do seems unnecessary to me. Why then?

I can't talk about it any more.

I love Russia.

In Paris, it seemed to me that I was discovering everything, above all a mastery of technique.

I convinced myself of this everywhere, in the museums and in the Salons.

Perhaps the East had strayed into my soul; or even the mad dog's bite [in childhood] had affected my mind.

It was not in technique alone that I sought the meaning of art then.

It was as if the gods had stood before me.

I no longer wanted to think about the Neo-classicism of David and Ingres, the Romanticism of Delacroix and the reconstruction of foregrounds by the disciples of Cézanne and Cubism.

I had the impression that we are still only roaming on the surface of matter, that we are afraid to plunge into chaos, to shatter and overthrow beneath our feet the familiar surface.

Marc Chagall was born in a poor Jewish family in Vitebsk, Russia, in 1887 and his early life there and his deeply religious background have provided the main source and inspiration for his art. In 1907 he went to St Petersburg to study painting and it was in the studio of Leon Bakst that he heard about the new artistic developments in Paris for the first time. In 1910 he left Russia and spent four years in Paris where he became friendly with many of the young revolutionary artists and poets, including Delaunay, La Fresnaye, Modigliani and Apollinaire. Though temporarily influenced by Cubism, Chagall only took from it what he needed to strengthen his own poetic, visionary style which with its rich colouring and highly fanciful arrangement of objects (Apollinaire used the word 'surnaturel' to describe it) made a deep impression on those around him. In 1914 he held his first exhibition, in Berlin, in the gallery of the magazine 'Der Sturm', which published many of his works. From 1914 to 1922 Chagall was again in Russia and after the Revolution was for a time Commissar of the Fine Arts at Vitebsk and later worked for the Jewish theatre in Moscow. He has lived in France again since 1923 with an interruption from 1941 to 1946 when he went to New York.

*Besides his paintings Chagall has also done important graphic work –
illustrations for Gogol's 'Dead Souls', La Fontaine's 'Fables', 'The Thousand
and One Nights' and the Bible – and monumental works for Israel and in Paris.
Although hailed in the 'thirties by the Surrealists, who were greatly influenced
by his fantasies, Chagall has maintained his independence and remained to this
day outside any particular school or movement.*

*From 1910 to 1914
Chagall worked in Paris
where he was tempo-
rarily influenced by Cub-
ism. In his 'Self-portrait
with Seven Fingers',
which was painted at this
period, though he has
adopted the Cubist style
he has not abandoned his
own personal iconography
and colouring.*

GEORGES BRAQUE ON THE BEGINNINGS OF CUBISM TO
DORA VALLIER IN CONVERSATION

1954

At that time I was very friendly with Picasso. Our temperaments were
very different, but we had the same idea. Later on it became clear,
Picasso is Spanish and I am French; as everyone knows, that means a
lot of differences, but during those years the differences did not count . . .
We were living in Montmartre, we used to meet every day, we used to
talk . . . In those years Picasso and I said things to each other that
nobody will ever say again, things that nobody could say any more, that
nobody would understand any longer . . . things that would be in-
comprehensible, and which gave us so much happiness . . . and it will
all come to an end with us.

It was rather like a pair of climbers roped together . . . We were
both working hard . . . Museums had ceased to interest us. We used to
go to exhibitions, but not as much as people suppose. We were very
self-contained more than anything else.

I felt dissatisfied with traditional perspective. Merely a mechanical
process, this perspective never conveys things in full. It starts from one
viewpoint and never gets away from it. But the viewpoint is quite
unimportant. It is as though someone were to draw profiles all his life,
leading people to think that a man has only one eye . . . When one got
to thinking like that, everything changed, you cannot imagine how
much! . . . What greatly attracted me – and it was the main line of
advance of Cubism – was how to give material expression to this new
space of which I had an inkling. So I began to paint chiefly still-lifes,
because in nature there is a tactile, I would almost say a manual, space.
I wrote about this moreover: 'When a still-life is no longer within
reach, it ceases to be a still-life.' . . . For me, that expressed the desire I
have always had to touch a thing, not just to look at it. It was that space
that attracted me strongly, for that was the earliest Cubist painting – the
quest for space. Colour played only a small part. The only aspect of
colour that concerned us was light. Light and space are connected,

aren't they, and we tackled them together . . . People called us abstract painters!

You know, when we were so friendly with Picasso, there was a time when we had difficulty in recognizing our own pictures. Later, when the revelation went deeper, differences appeared. Revelation is the one thing that cannot be taken from you. But before the revelation took place, there was still a marked intention of carrying painting in a direc-tion that would re-establish the bond between Picasso and ourselves. It's all a matter of one's age. At the age of twenty, the intelligence begins to develop first. Then come other factors. And that is why at that age the idea meant a lot to me. I considered that the painter's personality should be kept out of things, and therefore pictures should be anonymous. It was I who decided that pictures should not be signed, and for a time Picasso did the same. I thought that from the moment someone else could do the same as myself, there was no difference between the pictures and they should not be signed. Afterwards I realized it was not so and began to sign my pictures again. Picasso had begun again anyhow. I realized that one cannot reveal oneself without mannerisms, without some evident trace of one's personality. But all the same one should not go too far in that direction . . .

If I have called Cubism a new order, it is without any revolutionary ideas or any reactionary ideas . . . One cannot escape from one's own epoch, however revolutionary one may be. I do not think my painting has ever been revolutionary. It was not directed against any other kind of painting. I have never wanted to prove that I was right and someone else wrong . . . If there is a touch of reaction, since life imposes that, it is minute. And then it is so difficult to judge a thing historically, separated from its environment: it is the relationship between a man and what he does that counts. That's what is good and touches us.

If we had never met Picasso, would Cubism have been what it is? I think not. The meeting with Picasso was a circumstance in our lives. I even wrote apropos of poetry that it is 'circumstantial', and life is even more so.

Georges Braque (born 1882) *first learned to paint while apprenticed to a decorator, later studying at Le Havre and Paris. In 1906 he was working with the 'Fauve' group and met Picasso a year later, when the latter was studying Negro sculptures and painting 'Les Demoiselles d'Avignon'. This encounter was to have momentous results for modern painting. Braque is describing in this conversation how he and Picasso evolved a new approach to painting which became known as Cubism. From 1909 to the outbreak of the First World War Braque and Picasso worked together on Cubist lines in such close collaboration that it is often hard to distinguish their work of this period. When Braque resumed painting in 1917 after being wounded in the war, he tried to continue in the same manner at first, then evolved a freer style, in which he gave more play to colour and form and modified his geometrical approach.*

'. . . that was the earliest Cubist painting – the quest for space. Colour played only a small part.' *Braque's 'Girl with Guitar' was painted in 1913, and comes near the end of Cubism. A year later Braque joined the army and Picasso began to explore new styles.*

'Self-portrait' by Kokoschka. This painting, which shows the artist at the age of thirty-one, still belongs to his first, highly charged Expressionist period.

OSKAR KOKOSCHKA TO JAMES S. PLAUT

London, 13 May 1948

My dear Mr Plaut,

It is very kind of you to invite me to write a few words which can be used as a preface to the catalogue of the first representative exhibition of my paintings to be held in your country.

First of all, let me sincerely thank you for taking the initiative in this exhibition, and for devoting your time and energy to the task of making American art-lovers acquainted with what is more or less my life's work. Up to now, owing to two World Wars, it has been practically inaccessible to them.

Of course, visitors to Germany between the two wars became aware of the fact that Paris was not the only Mecca of modern art. But already before the outbreak of the Second World War, unfortunately, modern art was driven underground in a Germany overrun by Hitler. Thus the last time, for ten years or more, that my pictures could be shown was at the infamous Exhibition of Degenerate Art in Munich in 1937; this exhibition was visited by two and a half million sad Germans and

267

foreigners who came to say goodbye – as they must have thought then, for ever – to my fellow artists and me.

It is true that many a brave museum custodian did his best to protect my work by hiding it at great personal risk. Nevertheless a good third of it was lost later on, owing to the devastation of the war in Europe, and the upheaval of the liberation.

It was indeed a great effort on your part to have traced enough important paintings of mine to furnish characteristic examples of more or less all periods of my development.

Some visitors, well acquainted with modern art movements, may be puzzled to find that in my work there is none of the experimenting with all the different phases, from Impressionism, Pointillism, Cubism to non-objective art, which they are used to. The explanation is simple enough: I never intended to entertain my contemporaries with the tricks of a juggler, in the hope of being recognized as an original. I simply wanted to create around me a world of my own in which I could survive the progressive disruption going on all over the world. If this my world will survive me, so much the better. But I cannot *corriger la fortune*.

After forty years of work, however, it saddens me to have to listen to certain pronunciamentos of this, that or the other fashionable artist of today, abjuring his own work and denouncing modern art altogether, just because he finds himself in a blind alley. Unfortunately, such confessions of failure are bound to come just at a time when committee-controlled art makes news. I myself see no cause to retrace my steps. I shall not weary of testifying by the means given to me by nature and expressed in my art, in which only vision is fundamental, not theories. I consider myself responsible, not to society, which dictates fashion and taste suited to its environment and its period, but to youth, to the coming generations, which are left stranded in a blitzed world, unaware of the Soul trembling in awe before the mystery of life. I dread the future, when the growth of the inner life will be more and more hampered by a too speedy adaptation to a mechanically conceived environment, when all human industry is to be directed to fit in with the blue-prints.

Individually, no one will see his way before him. The individual will have to rely on hearsay for his knowledge, on second-hand experience, on information inspired by scientific inquiry only. None will have a vision of the continuity of life, because of the lack of spiritual means to aqcuire it.

For the growth of the inner life can never be brought into any scientific formula, whatever the technician and the scientist of the soul may try. The life of the soul is expressed by man in his art. (Do we not already need experts to lecture us on how to see a modern work of art?) The mystery of the soul is like that of a closed door. When you open it, you see something which was not there before.

Do not fear that I intend to lead you right off into metaphysics, whereas you only asked me for an introduction to the exhibition of my work. But if I were not a painter I could explain it all fully in words. So there we are.

Very sincerely yours,

Oskar Kokoschka

Oskar Kokoschka was born in Austria in 1886 of Czech and Austrian parents and received his artistic training in Vienna. His early portraits, passionate – even agonized – and profound in their psychological insight, made an immediate and violent impact upon the critics of the time. A leading modern painter at twenty-five, he also worked in other fields – poetry, drama and book illustration. He represented art in an avant-garde group which included the composer, Arnold Schönberg and the architect, Adolf Loos, and was invited by the editor of 'Der Sturm', Herwarth Walden, to collaborate with his group in Berlin. He was wounded in the war in 1916, then in 1918 settled in Dresden where he was called to a teaching post at the Academy. Between 1924 and 1931 he travelled widely in Europe, the Near East and North Africa, settled for a while in Prague in 1934, and in 1938 fled to London and later became naturalized. His aesthetic and political reactions to the dramatic events of his time were now more than ever reflected in his painting. In 1937 his work had been included in the notorious Exhibition of Degenerate Art together with paintings by Klee, Kandinsky, Nolde, Feininger and other outstanding artists.

Since the war Kokoschka has been teaching regularly at the summer school he founded in Salzburg – his 'School for Seeing' (Schule des Sehens). His

The Bride of the Wind' (1914), one of Kokoschka's masterpieces. The artist and the woman he loves are adrift in a boat on a stormy sea, the image of turbulent passion. 'It was the Baroque inheritance I took over', wrote Kokoschka.

reputation is now established as one of the great masters of this century. He has achieved a unique personal Expressionism which convinces by its intrinsic moral quality, rather than by relying on aesthetic appeal. His latest works continue to explore new possibilities, from large-scale allegories to magnificent landscapes or delicate flower-studies in watercolour, but his intense concern for human beings has never diminished. 'It is the psyche that speaks,' he has said, 'and all the artist can do is to bear witness to the vision within himself.'

JACKSON POLLOCK IN 'MY PAINTING'

1947

My painting does not come from the easel. I hardly ever stretch my canvas before painting. I prefer to tack the unstretched canvas to the hard wall or floor. I need the resistance of a hard surface. On the floor I am more at ease. I feel nearer, more a part of the painting, since this way I can walk round it, work from the four sides and literally be *in* the painting. This is akin to the method of the Indian sand painters of the West.

I continue to get further away from the usual painter's tools such as easel, palette, brushes, etc. I prefer sticks, trowels, knives and dripping fluid paint or a heavy impasto with sand, broken glass and other foreign matter added.

Action painting: a detail from 'Gothic' by Jackson Pollock, painted in 1944.

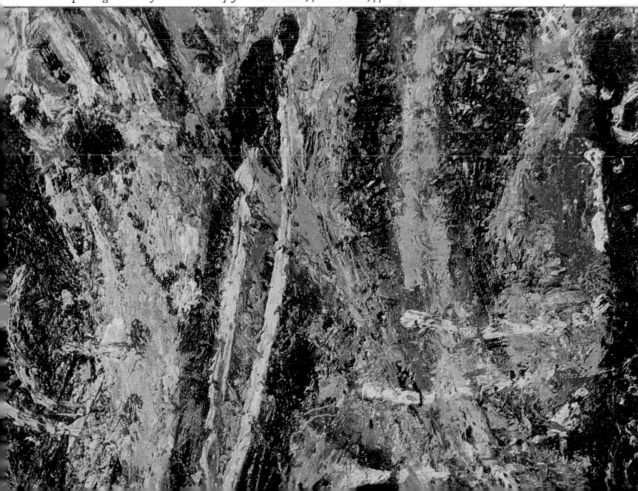

When I am *in* my painting I'm not aware of what I'm doing. It is only after a sort of 'get acquainted' period that I see what I have been about. I have no fears about making changes, destroying the image, etc., because the painting has a life of its own. I try to let it come through. It is only when I lose contact with the painting that the result is a mess. Otherwise there is pure harmony, an easy give and take, and the painting comes out well.

JACKSON POLLOCK IN HIS NARRATION FOR THE FILM 'JACKSON POLLOCK'

1951

I don't work from drawings or colour sketches. My painting is direct. ... The method of painting is the natural growth out of a need. I want to express my feelings rather than illustrate them. Technique is just a means of arriving at a statement. When I am painting I have a general notion as to what I am about. I *can* control the flow of paint: there is no accident, just as there is no beginning and no end.

Jackson Pollock (1912–1956) was the chief exponent of what is now termed 'Action painting'. After studying in Los Angeles and New York he turned to abstract art in 1940, evolving a highly personal technique which gave full freedom to spontaneity and accidental effects. After working at Springs, Long Island, for ten years, he was killed in a motor crash.

Pollock has exerted a great influence on many younger artists who share his predilection for unusual and often bizarre painting equipment, and for painting on lengths of canvas tacked on a floor rather than an easel. Since his death he has become an almost symbolic figure for the new movement in American art known as 'Abstract Expressionism' which has excited a great deal of controversy.

Notes to the Plates

Notes to the Plates

Notes to the Plates

Pages

13-15 WILLIAM BLAKE: Geoffrey Keynes (ed.), *Poetry and Prose of William Blake*, London and New York, 1943.

16-20 HENRY FUSELI: Walter Muschg (ed.), *Heinrich Füssli: Briefe*, Basle, 1942.

21-22 JOHN TRUMBULL: Theodore Sizer (ed.), *The Autobiography of Colonel John Trumbull, Patriot-Artist, 1756-1843*, New Haven and London, 1953.

23-24 RICHARD PARKES BONINGTON: A. Dubuisson, *Bonington*, Paris, 1927.

25-27 GOTTFRIED SCHADOW: Gottfried Schadow, 'Die Werkstätte des Bildhauers' in *Eunomia*, Berlin, October 1802.

28-29 PETER VON CORNELIUS: Ernst Förster, *Peter von Cornelius*, Berlin, 1874.

30-32 PHILIPP OTTO RUNGE: Philipp Otto Runge, *Hinterlassene Schriften*, Hamburg, 1840, 1841.

33-34 CASPAR DAVID FRIEDRICH: Else Cassirer (ed.), *Künstlerbriefe aus dem 19. Jahrhundert*, Berlin, 1923.

35-39 J. M. W. TURNER: Walter Thornbury, *The Life of J. M. W. Turner, R.A.*, London, 1877.

40-46 JOHN CONSTABLE: C. R. Leslie, *Memoirs of the Life of John Constable Esq., R.A.*, London, 1912.

48-54 JEAN AUGUSTE DOMINIQUE INGRES: Henri Delaborde, *Ingres: sa vie, ses travaux, sa doctrine*, Paris, 1870.

55-56 HIPPOLYTE FLANDRIN: Louis Flandrin, *Hippolyte Flandrin, sa vie et son oeuvre*, Paris, 1902.

57-61 PAUL GAVARNI: Edmond and Jules de Goncourt, *Gavarni. L'Homme et l'Œuvre*, Paris, 1873.

62-64 THÉODORE GÉRICAULT: Charles Clément, *Géricault*, Paris, 1868.

65-76 EUGÈNE DELACROIX: Philippe Burty (ed.), *Lettres de Eugène Delacroix*, Paris, 1880.

77-79 HONORÉ DAUMIER: Arsène Alexandre, *Honoré Daumier. L'Homme et l'Œuvre*, Paris, 1888.

80-82 CAMILLE COROT: Pierre Courthion, *Corot raconté par lui-même et par ses amis*, Geneva, 1946. Daniel Baud-Bovy, *Corot*, Geneva, 1957.

83-84 ADOLF VON MENZEL: Hugo von Tschudi, 'Aus Menzels jungen Jahren' in *Jahrbuch der Königlich Preuszischen Kunstsammlungen*, Berlin, 1905.

85-86 ARNOLD BÖCKLIN: Ferdinand Runkel and Carlo Böcklin, *Neben meiner Kunst. Flugstudien, Briefe und Persönliches von und über Arnold Böcklin*, Berlin, 1909.

87-88 HANS VON MARÉES: Julius Meier-Graefe, *Hans von Marées: sein Leben und sein Werk*, Munich, 1910.

89-91 WILHELM LEIBL: Julius Mayr, *Wilhelm Leibl: sein Leben und sein Schaffen*, Berlin, 1907.

92-94 DANTE GABRIEL ROSSETTI: George Birckbeck Hill (ed.), *Letters of Dante Gabriel Rossetti to William Allingham, 1854-1870*, London, 1897.

95-104 EDWARD BURNE-JONES: Lady Georgiana Burne-Jones, *Memorials of Edward Burne-Jones*, London, 1904.

105-109 WILLIAM MORRIS: J. W. Mackail, *The Life of William Morris*, London, 1901.

110-114 JEAN-FRANÇOIS MILLET: Alfred Sensier, *La Vie et l'Œuvre de J.-F. Millet*, Paris, 1881.

116-117 GUSTAVE COURBET: Pierre Courthion, *Courbet raconté par lui-même et par ses amis*, Geneva, 1948, 1950.

118-124 ÉDOUARD MANET: Étienne Moreau-Nelaton, *Manet raconté par lui-même*, Henri Laurens Éditeur, Paris, 1926.

Sources and References

Pages

126–132 CLAUDE MONET: Marthe de Fels, *La Vie de Claude Monet*, Paris, 1929.

133–139 PIERRE AUGUSTE RENOIR: Marthe de Fels, op. cit. Lionello Venturi, *Les Archives de l'Impressionisme*, Paris, 1939. Misia Sert, *Misia*, Paris, 1952.

140–143 AUGUSTE RODIN: Judith Cladel, *Rodin, sa vie glorieuse et inconnue*, Paris, 1936.

144–149 CAMILLE PISSARRO: John Rewald (ed.), *Camille Pissarro. Lettres à son fils Lucien*, Paris, 1950.

150–151 GEORGES SEURAT: John Rewald, *Georges Seurat*, Paris, 1948.

152–155 HENRI DE TOULOUSE-LAUTREC: 'Un Cahier Inédit de Toulouse-Lautrec' in *L'Amour de l'Art*, Paris, April 1951.

156–158 MAX LIEBERMANN: Else Cassirer, op. cit.

159–160 EDVARD MUNCH: Oslo Kommunes Kunstsamlinger, Munch-Museets Skrifter I, *Edvard Munchs Brev Familien*, Oslo, 1949. Translated by Stephen England.

161–167 PAUL GAUGUIN: Paul Gauguin, *Lettres de Paul Gauguin à Georges Daniel de Monfreid*, Paris, 1950.

168–173 VINCENT VAN GOGH: Vincent Van Gogh, *The Complete Letters of Vincent van Gogh*, New York and London, 1958.

174–177 JAMES ENSOR: Paul Haesaerts, *James Ensor*, London, 1957.

178–185 PAUL CÉZANNE: John Rewald (ed.), *Paul Cézanne. Correspondance*, Paris, 1937.

186–188 JAMES MCNEILL WHISTLER: James McNeill Whistler, *The Gentle Art of Making Enemies*, London, 1890.

189–192 WALTER RICHARD SICKERT: Osbert Sitwell (ed.), *A Free House! or, the Artist as Craftsman*, London, 1947.

Pages

193–195 AUBREY BEARDSLEY: R. A. Walker (ed.), *Letters from Aubrey Beardsley to Leonard Smithers*, London, 1937.

196–197 HENRY VAN DE VELDE: Else Cassirer, op. cit.

198–200 ANDRÉ DERAIN: M. de Vlaminck, *Derain. Lettres à Vlaminck*, Flammarion, Paris, 1909.

202–204 VASSILI KANDINSKY: Will Grohmann, *Wassily Kandinsky. Life and Work*, New York, 1959.

205–206 PAUL KLEE: Paul Klee, *Tagebücher 1898–1918*, Cologne, 1957.

207–208 FRANZ MARC: Franz Marc, *Briefe aus dem Felde*, Berlin, 1920.

209–212 ERNST BARLACH: Reinhard Piper, *Vormittag, Erinnerungen eines Verlegers*, Munich, 1947.

213–215 MAX BECKMANN: Reinhard Piper, *Nachmittag*, Munich, 1950. Benno Reifenberg and Wilhelm Hausenstein, *Max Beckmann*, Munich, 1955.

216–221 PAUL NASH: Paul Nash, *Outline, an autobiography, and other writings*, London, 1949.

222–230 ERNST LUDWIG KIRCHNER: E. L. Kirchner, *Briefe an Nele und Henry van de Velde*, Munich, 1961.

231–233 GIORGIO DE CHIRICO: Giorgio de Chirico, 'Le Mystère et la Création' in *The London Gallery Bulletin*, No. 6, London, 1938. Guido Ballo, *Modern Italian Painting: From Futurism to the present day*, London, 1958.

234–236 PIET MONDRIAAN: Piet Mondriaan, 'Extraits de lettres à Theo van Doesburg' in catalogue of the *De Stijl* Exhibition, Stedelijk Museum, Amsterdam, 1951. Translated by Ian F. Finlay. Michel Seuphor, *Piet Mondrian. Life and Work*, London, 1957.

Pages

237–241 HENRI MATISSE: 'Letter from Matisse' in an Exhibition Catalogue, Philadelphia Museum, 1948. By courtesy of Philadelphia Museum of Art.

242–246 PIERRE BONNARD: Tériade, 'Propos de Pierre Bonnard' and Angèle Lamotte, 'Le Bouquet de Roses' in *Verve*, Vol. V, Nos. 17 & 18, 'Couleur de Bonnard', Paris, 1947.

247–249 GINO SEVERINI: Gino Severini, 'Œuvres futuristes et cubistes' in an Exhibition Catalogue, Berggruen & Cie, Paris, 1956.

250–255 HENRY MOORE: David Sylvester (ed.), *Henry Moore. Volume One: Sculpture and Drawings 1921–1948*, London, 1957.

256–260 PABLO PICASSO: Christian Zervos, 'Conversation avec Picasso' in *Cahiers d'Art*, Vol. X, Paris, 1935. Translated by Elspeth A. Evans.

261–263 MARC CHAGALL: Marc Chagall, *Ma Vie*, Paris, 1931. Translated by Elspeth A. Evans.

264–266 GEORGES BRAQUE: Georges Braque, 'La Peinture et Nous. Propos de l'Artiste receuillis par Dora Vallier' in *Cahiers d'Art*, XXIXᵉ année, October 1954.

267–270 OSKAR KOKOSCHKA: James S. Plaut, *Oskar Kokoschka*, Boston and London, 1948.

271–272 JACKSON POLLOCK: Bryan Robertson, *Jackson Pollock*, London, 1960.

Index